THE GUN
THAT CHANGED
THE WORLD

To my daughter Elena

I was the slave of a single thought,
And a single passion consumed me.
M. I. Lermontov

THE GUN
THAT CHANGED
THE WORLD

MIKHAIL KALASHNIKOV

WITH

ELENA JOLY

TRANSLATED BY ANDREW BROWN

polity

First published in French as *Ma Vie en Rafales* by M. Kalashnikov with Elena Joly © Éditions du Seuil, May 2003. French edition originally edited by Patrick Rotman.

This English translation, Foreword to English edition and Glossary © Polity Press 2006.

All the photographs which appear in this book are from the personal archives of Mikhail Kalashnikov.

Polity Press
65 Bridge Street
Cambridge CB2 1UR, UK.

Polity Press
350 Main Street
Malden, MA 02148, USA

ISBN-10: 0-7456-3961-8
ISBN-13: 978-07456-3961-8
ISBN-10: 0-7456-3962-6 (pb)
ISBN-13: 978-07456-3962-6 (pb)

A catalogue record for this book is available from the British Library.

Typeset in 10.75 on 14 pt in Adobe Sabon
by Servis Filmsetting Ltd, Manchester
Printed and bound in Great Britain by MPG Books Ltd, Bodmin, Cornwall

For further information on Polity, visit our website: www.polity.co.uk

Ouvrage publié avec le concours du Ministère français chargé de la culture – Centre National du Livre.

Published with the assistance of the French Ministry of Culture – National Centre for the Book.

CONTENTS

ACKNOWLEDGEMENTS

Mikhail Kalashnikov would like to give his affectionate thanks to his daughter Elena for her help and support. Elena Joly would like to thank her friends Paul Perrot and Liane Willems, as well as her son Ivan Joly, for their help in the editing of the manuscripts.

FOREWORD TO THE ENGLISH EDITION: THE HISTORY AND WORKINGS OF THE AK-47

Before the nineteenth century, the standard infantry firearm was the muzzle-loading musket. The loading of these muskets from the front (the muzzle) was a fussy, time-consuming business, requiring the soldier to stand upright on the battle-field and go through the slow procedure of forcing gun-powder, wadding and a ball down the barrel with a long rod prior to firing. One estimate is that early matchlock muskets required 96 separate motions by the soldier for each round of firing. As they slowly loaded and fired, perhaps managing at most two rounds per minute, the soldiers with muskets needed to be protected against enemy cavalry and infantry charges. This required the deployment of soldiers with edged weapons – usually pikemen – interspersed among their vulnerable comrades who were busy loading and re-loading their muskets. The relatively simple technology of the bayonet, first used at the end of the seventeenth century, changed all of this. The French invention of the socket bayonet, which fixed over the end of a musket while still allowing firing, meant that the infantryman could stand alone.

If the inside of the barrel was rifled to give the bullet (or round) spin (and thus more accuracy), it was, technically, a muzzle-loading rifle. In the mid- to late nineteenth century, the advent of breech-loading rifles and new ammunition with more powerful propellant to drive the bullet revolutionized the firearm, allowing the infantryman to fire more quickly (up to 15 aimed rounds per minute) and in a prone position, as he did not have to stand up to load the weapon from the barrel. This new weapon was also much more accurate, with an effective range of 1,000 meters. By 1914, all major European armies had their own standard breech-loading infantry rifle, usually named after the factories that made them: Steyr Mannlicher (Austria), Mauser (Germany), Lee Enfield (Britain), Arisaka (Japan), Mosin-Nagant (Russia) and Springfield (USA).

The new breech-loading rifle was manually operated, with the soldier pushing each round individually into the chamber by means of a bolt action that moved the breechblock backwards and forwards, loading new bullets and ejecting spent bullet cases (or cartridges). Soon, soldiers fed these rifles manually, again using a bolt action, but from a magazine that could hold the bullets. This increased the speed of firing. These were powerful, heavy, often long, high-velocity weapons, capable of going through several bodies before stopping. The magazine-fed bolt-action rifle remained in use throughout World Wars I and II as the standard infantry weapon in all major armies. (Indeed, snipers still use such weapons today, as they are so accurate.) However, starting in the First World War, designers looked to modify the rifle in various ways.

In the 1880s, Hiram Maxim had invented a weapon that loaded and fired automatically – the machine gun. It used the gas from the explosion of the bullet in a reverse action to force back the mechanisms inside the weapon in a continuous action that reduced the gunner to the role of a machine operator. Fed by belts of ammunition stored in boxes, the machine gun was heavy, requiring a wheeled base and a team of soldiers to operate it. By the First World War, light machine guns such as the British Lewis gun fed by bigger magazines or strips of bullets were available. Designed to be fired in short bursts from a bipod, one man could carry the light machine gun into battle. It was, however, still fairly heavy and required supporting teams of soldiers to carry all the ammunition required. The need for even smaller, lighter weapons led to the deployment of the sub-machine gun, in operation from 1915 and widely used by the Germans at the end of the war. The problem with the sub-machine gun was its lack of accuracy and short range.

The need for an intermediate weapon between the rifle and machine gun on the one hand and the sub-machine gun on the other led designers to develop the assault rifle (sometimes called the automatic rifle). This would have the power of the rifle, the automatic capability of the machine gun, and the lightness of the sub-machine gun. It would fire an intermediate calibre bullet: lighter and less powerful than the standard rifle round, but more powerful than the sub-machine gun or pistol round. Such a weapon was ideal for the modern infantryman who needed maximum firepower, mass-produced and in a portable form. Combining these different functions was no easy task, and Mikhail Kalashnikov's fame comes from the way he went about tackling, and solving, the problem.

Kalashnikov improved and adapted existing technology and expertise for his AK-47. His skill lay in the way he did this, creating a weapon that met all the criteria asked of him and one which has stood the test of time and been copied by numerous other weapons designers. Kalashnikov used the gas principle from the machine gun as the starting point for the AK-47. When the first bullet is fired by a small pin being forced into the back of it, the gas from the explosion in the base of the metal case (or cartridge) that holds the bullet follows it down the barrel. It cannot go backwards, as the breech/chamber from which the bullet has been fired is sealed by the bullet's metal case and a locking mechanism on the bolt carrier. Before the bullet leaves the end of the barrel, a small hole in the top of the barrel fairly near the muzzle allows some of the gas travelling behind the bullet into a short chamber that lies on top of the barrel. The concentration of gas in this chamber forces back a long rod (or piston) on the bolt carrier. This pushes back the bolt carrier. As it moves back, working against a returning spring, it slides on two grooves in the receiver part of the weapon and pulls back a rotating bolt. While Kalashnikov did not invent the rotating bolt, he adapted it to great effect in the AK-47, and in his autobiography he is rightly proud of the way he made it work so well. As the rotating bolt is twisted and pulled back inside the bolt carrier, it ejects the spent metal bullet cartridge (or jacket), forces back the hammer of the trigger (thus re-cocking the weapon) and then returns forward under pressure of the return spring. As it does so, the rotating bolt now swivels back to its original position; in doing so, it picks up another round from the magazine and locks itself tightly into the chamber, ready for the next round to be fired. If the soldier has his weapon set to automatic, this process is repeated all over again. This cycle of firing and reloading does, of course, happen very, very quickly. All the soldier has to do is keep his finger on the trigger and he can fire all 30 rounds in the AK's curved magazine. This is not, however, best practice, as long bursts, while technically possible, over-heat the barrel and will lead to bullets 'spraying out' inaccurately. Soviet/Russian infantrymen were (indeed, still are) taught to fire short bursts of 2–3 rounds from the Kalashnikov.

Kalashnikov's design is beautifully simple. Not only are the moving parts kept to a bare minimum, but the bolt carrier that is doing the work is located high up the receiver on two grooves (Kalashnikov describes his bolt carrier/moving parts as 'floating'). This means that any dust or grit that gets into the receiver where all the key moving parts are located should do little damage, as the vibration caused by firing the weapon will mean that they fall harmlessly down to the bottom of the receiver. While modern Western assault rifles work on similar principles, they are far more complicated to operate and, although more accurate than the AK-47, are also more likely to jam and more difficult to strip down and clean, especially when in battle. The Kalashnikov is a basic, functional weapon designed for armies of peasants. It is very easy, even for a layperson with no weapons training, to break down a Kalashnikov into its component parts – not something one would say about, for instance, the British army's current SA-80 assault rifle that is very difficult to take apart. The curved magazine, an integral part of the iconic image of the AK, is a result of the bullets being bottle-nosed and so best stored in a curve.

The AK-47 was bored for a 7.62 mm diameter round. In the 1950s, the Soviets modernized the weapon (as the AKM) and in 1974 the Soviets introduced the AK-74 with a smaller 5.45 mm round. The basic design, however, remained the same, and in its variant forms the AK carried on in use in the USSR and in Soviet satellite states where it was mass-produced in local factories. As he never patented his weapon, Kalashnikov claims that he never made any money from his design. It is ironic that the American, Eugene Stoner, the inventor of the American M-16 automatic (assault) rifle – the standard infantry weapon in the US army – died relatively unknown but a millionaire, whereas Kalashnikov is relatively poor but famous the world over.

As well as the millions of AK-47s produced by Soviet satellite states and in illegal arms factories, the Israelis, Finns and South Africans all copied Kalashnikov's design for their standard infantry rifles. The AK does have its drawbacks. It is not terribly accurate, is effective only to about 400 metres, and the safety device on the right-hand side that goes from 'off' to 'automatic' to 'semi-automatic' makes a loud click as it is made ready to fire. These are, however, minor defects in a weapon renowned for its extreme ruggedness, simplicity of operation and maintenance, and unsurpassed reliability even in the worst conditions possible. Indeed, the AK is the only firearm ever that is depicted on a national flag – that of Mozambique where it symbolizes liberation. It also appears on the flag of the Lebanese political party, Hizbollah. While the Russian army is now working on new assault rifles such as the AN-94, the AK remains the main weapon used in the Russian army almost 60 years after Kalashnikov first invented it. Moreover, with the phasing out of the old standard rifle (except for specialized sniper work) the assault rifle principle embodied in the Kalashnikov has become the standard pattern for infantry weaponry today.

Matthew Hughes
Brunel University

PREFACE: THE TERROR AND THE GLORY

There are a dozen or so words that are the same in every language of the world. Everyone knows them, from Chilean peasants to Japanese workers, from English city folk to Afghan mountain-dwellers. They include the words 'taxi', 'radio', 'Coca-Cola' – and 'Kalashnikov'. The Russian name that is uttered most often, worldwide, isn't Lenin, Stalin or Gorbachev, but Kalashnikov. And the word points to a significant reality: between 60 and 80 million Kalashnikovs are in circulation, in all five continents.

In Izhevsk, an isolated town in the depths of the Urals, a 'young man', 83 years old, opens the security door to his house, grumbling, 'These days they make doors out of steel. You have to defend yourself against burglars, hooligans, bandits of every kind. It wasn't like that in Soviet times!'

Defend, defend yourself: the favourite words of Mikhail Timofeyevich Kalashnikov. Throughout his life – and what an extraordinary life it has been – he has had to defend himself against his country just as much as he fought in its defence. He was at one and the same time the victim and the hero of a terrible period in history.

The man who opens his door to me is very elegantly dressed, not in honour of our meeting, but out of everyday habit. His apartment is spacious, pleasant and kept immaculately tidy. Kalashnikov thinks it is important to have beautiful things around him; above all, he believes in order. Order is one of the keywords of his destiny.

He is very Russian, and gives me an 'old-style' welcome, offering me a choice of tea, fish soup (his speciality) or vodka. He isn't tall, but stands so upright that other people seem smaller when they are with him. His thick, white hair is carefully combed. He looks much more like a gentleman than a muzhik.

Kalashnikov's piercing gaze, evidence of a certain wariness, seems to weigh up his visitors. But he never stops telling jokes. 'There are some things that are so serious', he says, 'that you can only talk about them humorously.' I am surprised at the extensive culture this self-taught man displays: he recites poetry, sings Béranger,[1] comes out with witty puns and laughs heartily. He is curious about everything: things, people and their lives, including mine. He's also a passionate man: when he relates a memory that he holds dear, he grows animated, straightens up, gesticulates and puts everything he's got into his lines, like a good actor. But you have to manage to kindle the sacred flame within him, for if you don't, you'll never get a thing out of him: Kalashnikov will shut up like a tank whose hatch has been battened down.

There's no affectation and no pretentiousness in this general: just plain talking. If you know anything about the tendency of great men in the Soviet regime to indulge in political cant and bureaucratic haughtiness, you might expect the worst when it's the most highly decorated man in Russia that you're talking to. But Kalashnikov isn't big-headed, and in any case he's more original than that, and full of surprises.

* * *

I've known Lena, his daughter, for a long time: she often comes to see me in Paris. One day she told me the poignant story of her father and his family. I suddenly realized that, behind the notorious weapon, there was a man whose destiny had been quite extraordinary – a tragic and terribly Russian destiny.

In the West, nobody knows this man's story: people are not even aware that he is still alive. The idea of interviewing Kalashnikov was alluring. It wasn't easy to obtain his agreement, but in the end I gained his trust. This book reflects our conversations: I have respected Kalashnikov's original style and simply incorporated my questions into his narrative so as to give it a chronological structure.

For an English-language reader who may not be particularly familiar with the stormy course of Soviet history, I have included, at the start of every chapter, a few key facts that will enable Kalashnikov's personal history to be set within the wider history of his time.

Mikhail Kalashnikov was born into a peasant family in 1919, in the middle of the Civil War. His mother had 18 children, of whom only 8 survived. In 1930, a black year for Soviet peasantry, the Kalashnikovs were hit by Stalin's repression and the process of 'dekulakization'. Mikhail (Misha) didn't learn about the harshest periods of Soviet history from books: he lived through them.

At the age of 11, Misha thus found himself being sent to Siberia, with his parents and four of his brothers. He was already demonstrating exceptional obstinacy and perseverance: on two occasions, he escaped from the place to which they had been deported, refusing to accept the destiny that had been meted out to him, and returned on foot to his home village, more than 600 miles away.

One day he found a rusty, out-of-order German pistol. He spent whole days trying to mend it, and realized that he had discovered his vocation. He was denounced to the militia and arrested. He was pressed to hand over his pistol, but Misha denied everything: in those days you didn't know where a confession might lead. After three days of interrogation, he was released: he fled from his village and set off for Kazakhstan, where his life as a technician began.

Called up for military service in 1938, Kalashnikov became a mechanic on a tank. This meant he could openly show his talents as a weapons constructor: he was only 20 when he invented some original new fittings for tanks. These came to the attention of no less a person than a highly appreciative General Zhukov.

When war broke out, he left for the front; a few months later, he was seriously wounded during the celebrated battle of Bryansk, fighting against German panzers. After seven days spent wandering around behind German lines, he was miraculously saved, once again thanks to his obstinacy, and ended up for a long period in a Soviet hospital. These episodes would not be out of place in the best war novels. 'And here, in spite of the pain of my injury, I was obsessed night and day by a single thought: inventing a weapon to beat the fascists.' Thus it was that, after five years of unremitting work, the celebrated assault rifle, the AK-47, was born.

This famous inventor never completed his studies at secondary school. 'I was a born inventor', he says. 'My universities were books.' In 1949, at the age of 29, he was awarded the Stalin Prize, which marked a real turning-point in his life: the outcast now joined the world of the privileged.

Elected six times to the Supreme Soviet, Kalashnikov entered the Holy of Holies, the Kremlin, but he never really fitted in with the Communist political elite. He remained a somewhat distant observer of the real struggles for power.

Mikhail Gorbachev's perestroika, of which Kalashnikov never approved, did nonetheless enable him to speak – at long last – openly about his past, and to travel the world. This gave him the chance to meet, among others, his American rival Eugene Stoner, with whom he amicably discussed the millions of soldiers to be seen, throughout the world, equipped with Kalashnikovs and M-16s. Paradoxically, while the USSR, despite being a collectivist society, had baptized the weapon with the name of its inventor, America, the land of individualism, had concealed the inventor's name behind an anonymous label.

In his own words, Kalashnikov has devoted his whole life to his weapon. From the age of 20, he was obsessed by just one idea, one project: to create and develop the best weapon in the world to defend his country. This do-it-yourself mechanic of genius claims the title of 'inventor' and declares that he will have nothing to do with any of the weapons markets. He proudly proclaims that he's never earned a kopek, anywhere or from anyone, from the sale of his weapons. The idea of patenting his invention, once the war that had ravaged his country was over, never even entered his head.

*   *   *

The creation of the AK-47 was no miracle: it was the result of prolonged work, marked by humiliating setbacks that Kalashnikov overcame thanks to the same notorious peasant obstinacy that had already enabled him to escape a humdrum existence in his childhood. The idea of a new weapon haunted him for five years, from the time when he was lying wounded in hospital and starting to sketch out his first ideas, to the glorious day when the Main Artillery Directorate accepted his first prototype.

How did this obscure 26-year-old sergeant, who wasn't even an engineer, manage to outstrip several excellent inventors, certain of them personally admired by Stalin himself? The answer lies precisely in the fact that Kalashnikov was a soldier from the ranks and a peasant: the strength of his weapon resided in its simplicity and reliability, and not in any sophistication. The AK was created in an empirical fashion, proceeding by 'trial and error' rather than any scientific methodology. Katya, the woman who eventually became his wife, would be drawing the different parts of the prototype when he had finished putting them together with his own hands, in his workshop! The story of Kalashnikov and his golden fingers is rather reminiscent of how Bill Gates or Steve Jobs began – those obsessive young men developing the future of the computer industry in their mythical garages.

According to specialists, the originality that meant the AK could triumph over its competitors lay in the rotary piece of the breechblock, lodged in the gas reclamation cylinder above the barrel. The dream of perpetual motion, which the young Misha had been pursuing ever since the dark period of his Siberian exile, consisted in the quest for this innovative mechanism that would enable the rifle to fire in bursts.

No less innovative was the principle underlying the way the pieces were assembled. Instead of being pressed together in a compact block, they were spaced out and separated, as if hanging in air. This enabled the Kalashnikov to be dragged through dust, mud and water during combat: it didn't let its soldier down and was always at his service.

Although Stalin awarded the prize that bears his own name (the highest distinction of that time) to Kalashnikov in 1949, the leader of the USSR still did not appreciate the weapon as highly as he should have done: several years later, the army as a whole had still not adopted the new assault rifle. In the parades on Red Square, soldiers would still march with the Simonov rifles that had shown their mettle during the war.

On Stalin's death in 1953, most soldiers had yet to set eyes on an AK-47. Nikita Khrushchev had other priorities: the H-bomb and rockets. Even today, Kalashnikov cannot forgive him for having treated firearms as 'techniques from the age of cave-men'.

But throughout these years, in spite of everyone, in his factory in the depths of the Urals, the peasant inventor was developing and improving his work. The huge factory in Izhevsk, which had already been building cannon to fight off Napoleon, had produced as many as 12,000 automatic weapons per day during World War II. It was here that mass production of the Kalashnikov began – that legendary weapon that was to meet with an unequalled success right across the globe.

Toward the end of the 1950s, after 10 years of a well-kept blanket of secrecy cast over the AK and its ammunition, the West was forced to face the facts: the USSR possessed the best combat weapon in the world. And the Vietnam War, a few years later, would bring confirmation of this. Gradually, the whole Soviet army, followed by all the armies of the Warsaw Pact, were equipped with the AK-47 and its spin-offs. During the 1960s, with the Vietnam War and various liberation movements, the weapon assumed strong ideological and symbolic connotations. The legend of the Kalashnikov was born.

In 2000, the French daily newspaper *Libération* indulged in the game of drawing up a list of the 'objects of the twentieth century'. The Kalashnikov has a distinguished place there, together with television, antibiotics and bras.

*   *   *

So what role exactly did the Kalashnikov play in the history of the twentieth century or, more precisely, the second half of the century? What will weigh most heavily in the balance? Did the 'Kalash' contribute more to the liberation of the world's different peoples, or to their oppression?

In the 1950s, both of these two movements were at work: Cuba on the one side, and Budapest on the other. Shortly afterwards, during the Vietnam War, so disastrous for America's image, the AK, superior to the M-16, contributed decisively to the victory of the Vietcong.

Until 1968, revolutionary, anti-colonial and anti-imperialist romanticism gained ground in the Third World and among young Westerners. This was the period when demonstrators almost everywhere would brandish the portraits of Che Guevara and Ho Chi Minh. The AK, visible in all the photos in the hands of every hero, was at the heart of every liberation struggle. 'The Kalashnikov', Yasser Arafat proclaimed at the time, 'is the honour of our fighters everywhere!'

After Indochina and Egypt, Cuba and Palestine, a large part of the Third World erupted into violence. But the Soviet Union no longer played a predominant role in the spread of the AK and its imitations. It was China that took over this role.

In August 1968, with the Soviet intervention in Prague, a less glorious period began. The 1970s and 1980s would be marked by the rising tide of international terrorism. There was a spate of spectacular and deadly terrorist attacks throughout those dark and oppressive years: they horrified the world. In the hands of Palestinian, German, Japanese, and Italian terrorists, the already familiar outline of the AK could be seen – to the great despair of Kalashnikov himself. 'I hope that I will be remembered as the man who invented a weapon to defend the borders of his own country, and not a weapon for terrorists.'

Unfortunately, this was just the start of the inventor's nightmares. More or less everywhere, savage wars broke out: combatants from every camp, armed with Kalashnikovs, engaged in hand-to-hand fighting: Iran, Iraq, Lebanon, Angola, Ethiopia, Cambodia. The AK and its spin-offs were eventually the weapon of choice for 55 regular armies, plus an indeterminate number of movements of the most varied ideologies, or even with no ideology at all.

And things went from bad to worse: with the war in Afghanistan, the Kalashnikov was turned against the Soviet soldiers. Shortly afterwards, various conflicts started to tear apart the USSR, and finally Russia itself, with the AK still playing a major role. And the dramatic events in Chechnya are a reminder that the story is far from over.

For a long time, the AK has escaped not only from its inventor's control, but also from that of Soviet leaders. 'The weapon', Kalashnikov says, 'now has a life of its own, quite independent of my will.' The man has been outstripped by his own creation.

*   *   *

In this book, the reader will find nothing of this story, or next to nothing. Kalashnikov seems to have erected a wall between himself and certain topics, so as to evade questions on issues that are too sensitive. It isn't easy to be forthcoming when you have been subject to secrecy all your life.

Kalashnikov was a doubly secretive man: he concealed his past, and he himself was concealed from the eyes of the outside world – to such an extent, in fact, that the little Republic of Udmurtia, where he lived and worked, was forbidden to outsiders.

These days, he thinks that it's for politicians to accept responsibility for what happened. Unlike Andrei Sakharov, the creator of the Soviet bomb, who was assailed by doubts and eventually turned against his masters, Kalashnikov made the once-for-all decision that he had no control of events and confined himself to the role of a pure technician. As one of his favourite proverbs puts it, 'where the goat is tied, there she must graze'.

And yet the young Misha had all the makings of a rebel. He risked everything to flee from his Siberian exile, and escaped prison, the Gulag, and even death by the skin of his teeth. In the bloody chaos of the USSR of the 1930s, he would not have been the first person to disappear without leaving any trace.

This society violently rejected him and his family. 'We're not going to call you "comrades" any more, and you don't have the right to call us by that name', they were told on arrival in Siberia. This profound trauma still hurts him even today, even though he has tried to repress it and in spite of half a century of honours lavished on him by the state. Kalashnikov wanted to do more and perform better than everyone else, so as to be a 'comrade' just like them. And what could be more useful to his threatened country than to give it a new weapon to defend itself with?

But serving his country meant first and foremost serving Stalin. It was a time for blind fanaticism. 'Stalin was God', and Stalinism at its apogee didn't teach people to think, but to believe. Soviet deputies, of whom Kalashnikov was one, applauded their Guide to the point of exhaustion, since none of them dared be the first to stop clapping.

This was a fanaticism mingled with terror. Kalashnikov was never free from fear, obliged as he was to conceal for more than 50 years his past as an 'enemy of the people', since any such admission would have meant that every door was slammed in his face.

In any case, we might well learn one day, from some dossier in the archives, that the Party was aware of his secret:

Stalin had a perverse liking for keeping useful people under his thumb by holding them by their hidden weak points. In this way he turned people into cogs in his machine, since they owed everything to him – their careers, their fame, their lives. In the sixteenth century, La Boétie had already described these mechanisms of voluntary servitude.[2]

Thus it was that the young rebel became a *homo sovieticus* and remains so to this day. Did this man, with his exceptional destiny, a man who changed the history of the world, pass by that history without ever really seeing it?

Elena Joly

TREADING A PATH OF
PAIN AND SORROW

Kalashnikov's whole existence was marked by 'dekulakiza-tion': the members of his family, exiled to Siberia in appalling conditions and deprived for long years of their civic rights, were forced to undergo many humiliations, privations and sorrows.

In 1929, Stalin decreed total collectivization. Peasants were obliged to serve in the kolkhozes: if they refused, they were deported. The authorities began by getting rid of the better off (known as kulaks): they were hostile to this system and might have influenced the others, so they were sent to Siberia and other regions in the north. Through this action, the state was pursuing a double objective: populating almost desert-like regions, and acquiring a cheap labour force that could cut down trees and work in agriculture and metallurgy.

Between 1930 and 1933, this mass deportation was at its height and affected about 1,400,000 kulak peasants. From 1930 onwards, the kolkhozes were subjected to 'enforced organization'. Dekulakization was the means by which this collectivization process was imposed. In 1934, at the end of the first five-year plan, two-thirds of peasant families had been brought into the kolkhozes – but at what a price! The peasantry put up fierce resistance and there was massive migration from the countryside to the town, which led to grave problems of food and lodging.

Another problem was the mass slaughter of livestock, sometimes organized by the kulaks themselves. The 'richest' of them tried by this means to enter the category of the 'serednyaks' (peasants of middling wealth) so as to avoid ending up in Siberia. As a result, the number of heads of livestock dropped by half.

Throughout these years, Russia exported a huge quantity of wheat that could have been used to avoid famine and save countless people. In addition, the authorities confiscated bread from the kolkhozes and individual homes at a time when the populace was starving to death. By 1933, famine was ravaging Russia, the Ukraine in particular: ten million people were affected.

The Party Secretary in one of the affected regions relates in one of his letters how, in his constituency, it was not rare to see a kolkhoz labourer forced to work in such a state of exhaustion that he collapsed and died out in the middle of the fields. This work was all but unpaid. In 1932, the 'passport system' tied the peasant to his kolkhoz, and forbade him from leaving it. The deportees were administered by the GPU (State Political Administration – the ancestor of the notorious KGB), and their situation was similar to that of the Gulag. They were sent to live in the Urals, Siberia, Kazakhstan and Central Asia. They worked with non-political and political prisoners on the canals linking the White Sea to the Baltic and the Moskva to the Volga, and also constructed various dams. This massive influx of forced labour caused terrible difficulties during their transport, and subsequently led to a shortage in lodging, foodstuffs and equipment.

Within four years, a quarter of these displaced persons perished as a result of epidemics, famine and back-breaking labour. Collectivization took a dreadful toll. It is estimated that the peasant world lost 25 million individuals.

The years 1928 and 1929 comprised a second revolution, which completely transformed the way of life of the Russian peasants. Even now, its repercussions continue to affect Russia's economy.

SON OF A KULAK

Although I have a typically Russian face, my family's roots go back to the Kuban region, near the Caucasus mountains. The name of my ancestors, Cossacks who were 'as free as the wind' (as the saying had it), was Kalashnik. In the middle of the nineteenth century, when they became peasants, they chose to Russianize their name to Kalashnikov.

My mother, Aleksandra Frolovna Kaverina, born in 1884, came from a relatively well-off family, which included several priests. She herself was very pious. At the turn of the century, she married Timofei Aleksandrovich Kalashnikov, a poor but hard-working peasant, a year older than herself.

In 1910, when Tsar Nicholas II decided to grant the peasants arable lands in the Altai region,[1] my parents decided to settle there with their three children. It was here that I was born and bred, in the village of Kurya. My mother gave birth to me in our izba [cottage: Tr.] just as she was bringing in pails full of water. She hardly had time to put them down before I was born. My mother had 18 children, of whom only eight survived.

I often think back to my childhood. When the October Revolution broke out, my family was neither rich nor poor. My parents already had six children, all of them accustomed from a very young age to hard peasant toil: it was necessary if we were to survive. I was the eighth child, born in 1919. Our house, a traditional log-cabin izba, had a living-room, a kitchen and an entry hall. Although there was a wood-plank floor in the main room, the clay floor in the entrance hall and the kitchen betrayed my parents' Cossack origins. There were so many of us that the family table wasn't big enough for us all: our grandparents presided at the two ends, my parents and the biggest children squeezed onto the benches together. As for the youngest, they sat on the ground with their mess tins on their knees.

This didn't prevent us from observing the religious rituals scrupulously, and no one would have dared to start the meal without first mumbling the prayers. In the same way, before we went to bed, we all knelt under the icon. As far as I was concerned, even when I was just a kid, I prayed out of obedience, not out of any sense of conviction.

From my tenderest years onward, I loved making all sorts of objects with my own hands – little houses, miniature windmills. My father often used to say of me, 'Misha's going to be a builder! Don't stop him working on his little houses!'

I went down with every childhood illness you can possibly imagine. Sometimes I had two or three at once. When I was 6, they very nearly buried me. I'd stopped breathing. My mother brought a hen's feather up to my nose, and there was no reaction on my part. So my parents resigned themselves and summoned the carpenter to make the coffin. But no sooner did he start hammering and banging with his tools than I came round. According to the family legend, the carpenter exclaimed: 'So young, and he's already pulling a fast one! *He's* a good actor, and no mistake!'

Although I was sickly and ailing, I always wanted to play with my big brothers and their mates. In winter, one of my brothers managed to make me some wooden ice skates. But when I went skating on the frozen river, I almost ended up there for good. I was walking across the ice and it broke: I found myself in a hole of ice-cold water. I was wearing an extremely heavy coat at the time, and it dragged me to the bottom. It was my brother who saved my life: he pulled me out with more-than-human strength. And the following summer, I almost drowned in that very same river. I have to admit I couldn't swim – actually, I still can't! I've had a sort of lifelong phobia for water ever since.

When I was little, I also had smallpox – I still have a few traces on my face. Much later, when I went to Moscow for the first time, I immediately made an appointment at a beautician's, but I gave a false name, Ivanov – I didn't want anyone to find out that I frequented places like that, even though the risk was pretty minimal! In the end I didn't dare show up.

At the age of 7, I started to work in the fields. Every summer I was 'lent out' to neighbours for their less onerous agricultural chores.

My parents didn't exactly have fun-filled lives: they never stopped working. But my mother loved life and she enjoyed a joke. She was as tender-hearted as my father was severe. I had the impression I was her favourite child, but maybe this was an illusion.

They had practically no education. My mother was completely illiterate, and my father had left school after two or three years of studies. But at home there were always newspapers and reviews strewn around. My father would read them as soon as he had a bit of free time.

During the long winter nights, my father's friends would come to our house; they told stories, sometimes until daybreak. We children listened to them, pretending to be asleep. I can also remember tranquil evenings: my mother would be spinning wool, helped by my sisters, who were much older than me; my father would be resting; my brother Viktor would read out some poetry by Nekrasov, our favorite poet.[2] My sister Gasha, who had an incredible memory, knew a lot of it off by heart, and sometimes amused herself by carrying on, from memory. My father hummed quietly, then my mother and my sisters joined in, and the whole family started to sing, apart from me, since I had no voice and no ear for music. It was very cold outside, but inside, thanks to our good old stove, we felt nice and warm. I can still feel that warmth.

My parents treated all the children the same way, even if the younger ones were obviously pampered more than the older ones. Naturally, we copied our big brothers and sisters, who taught us a great deal, including reading and writing. As a result, by the time I arrived at school, I could already read and write. My parents demanded that we should be high-flyers at school, and my mother was very proud of my successes.

My first school-mistress was an extraordinary woman. She looked after us even outside school hours. She came to see us at our homes, and spent a long time talking to our parents. At school, another thing we learned was how to raise livestock 'scientifically'. Each of us had to raise an animal. I was given a little calf, and I took really good care of it.

I loved my school, my teacher and my family: I was a happy child. I am grateful to my parents for having brought me into the world, and for the opportunity to live on this earth.

* * *

Along came 1929. People in the countryside lived in constant fear of informers. We schoolchildren were aware of everything that happened in our village. For certain peasant households, the events of those distant years were really catastrophic. Party delegates came more and more often to hold meetings for the 'indigent peasants', as they were called. At these meetings, they would draw up lists in which the peasants were classified into three categories: poor peasants (bednyaki), peasants of middling income (serednyaki) and well-off peasants or 'kulaks'.[3] Those who fell into the third category had to be deported to Siberia and their property was confiscated. Those stormy meetings lasted all night. If anyone opposed the fact that a family had been placed in the third category, and claimed that the household in question could hardly be considered as well-off, he was immediately accused of being in cahoots with the money-bags. Just try and defend your neighbour in conditions like that!

What a storm of tears and laments there was when they came to confiscate everything considered superfluous from a peasant household! A peasant never has any surplus. The Party delegates soon decided the matter: 'You have no right to possess this or that'. And they confiscated everything: livestock, poultry, wheat and even potatoes. They rummaged around everywhere in case the owner had had the gumption to hide his goods away.

The children knew which of the villagers supported the way those who possessed more livestock than was permitted were stripped of their civic rights and deported to Siberia. As a result, there was trouble and strife at school too, with rich and poor set against one another. The exchange of insults and reproaches sometimes led to a general scrap. The children hurled abuse at each other, and called each other 'kulaks' and 'exploiters'. Those who were the objects of these insults were always viewed as having started these scraps, even if they were only defending themselves.

But was there really such a difference between rich and poor? The 'rich' generally had big families, and so they had to raise more livestock. So how could you judge?

One day, as soon as we arrived at school, the teacher told us that four of our schoolmates had been deported to Siberia with their parents during the night. We were dumbstruck at the news, and felt a sense of guilt. I was all the more sorry in that Zina, my little girlfriend, was also on her way to Siberia. Several times a day I would pass in front of her windows, hoping for a miracle. Perhaps I'll see her sweet face and lovely smile again, I thought. Alas! Such was the tragic end of my first childhood love. Poor Zina! How did your long journey into the unknown end? Whatever became of you?

It was almost the end of the school year, and we were getting ready for the springtime work out in the fields. Once again I would be looking after our neighbour's horses. He was very satisfied with the work I'd done the year before, and sang my praises to my father, who was highly delighted.

During the periods of seasonal work, peasant families would share out their tasks: the boys looked after the horses, and the girls took care of the youngsters while their parents were working in the fields. Rare were the households that could manage without this mutual aid.

You have to have experienced agricultural labour to have any idea of the harshness of this back-breaking chore, those never-ending days when swarms of mosquitoes, horseflies and midges harass men and beasts.

The next year, 1930, brought misfortune to my family. I was 11. Several months had gone by since the deportation of the first group of peasant families. We were starting to receive letters from the deportees. It was impossible to read the accounts of the terrible trials and tribulations endured by those poor folk without weeping: the rigours of the journey along impassable roads, the coarse brutality of their guards, the illnesses, the hostility of the inhabitants of those Siberian villages at the back of beyond, who viewed all these new arrivals and their famished rabble of kids with mistrust.

In my school at Kurya, the peasants' children continued to scrap, even more than before, and long-standing friendships dissolved for obscure reasons. The kids were like a barometer, able to feel the approaching storm.

Once again, just like the previous year, Party representatives arrived in our village to continue the work of expropriating the kulaks and preparing to deport a new group of peasant families to the furthest reaches of the taiga.

This time, our name appeared on the blacklist of kulaks. I'll never forget that terrible winter's day. Our farmyard was overrun by herds of cows and sheep that had been seized from the peasants who were about to be deported – all those animals who could smell death in the air and careered round and round, looking for an escape.

Suddenly, a few men, big strapping fellows, came into our house armed with axes and knives. And for the first time, I saw how you could fell a huge bull with just one blow of an axe. The beast collapsed to its knees or toppled over to one side, and they immediately slit its throat. The bull tried vainly to get back to its feet. Its blood came spurting out in torrents. Once the cows and sheep had been cut up, their innards were slung over the fence. Calves and lambs, still alive, went around paddling in this mess. It was just horrible to see it! But those butchers just roared with laughter as they felled another pregnant cow. They said, 'This way, we'll spare the owners all the bother of rearing the calf!'

Finally, they slaughtered our ewes. I hid behind a window to watch, fascinated: it was an utterly crazy scene, beyond all understanding. When it was all over, our farmyard was a dreadful sight. My father ordered us to cover all that blood with a layer of snow. But there was blood everywhere, and in order to clean it up, we had to fetch snow from our vegetable garden and even from our neighbours.

Soon, as we knew, it would be our turn to go. One of my sisters, Niura, had been married for a year to a poor, hard-working peasant, but another sister, Gasha, had married one of the most fervent Communists in the village: he was the leader of the local atheists' association. He knew that our father had long since been designated for deportation, and he had forbidden his wife to come and see us.

In our house, that had once been so bustling and full of life, the silence weighed heavily on us. We exchanged a few words in hushed tones. Even the cock no longer dared to crow in the farmyard.

Then came the day of departure. Two sleighs, harnessed up and filled with hay, halted outside our home. Then we gathered everything we could carry and set off into the unknown, abandoning our house, with other families of kulaks.

My sister Gasha, in spite of her husband's forbidding her to do so, ran along behind the sleigh, sobbing and moaning like an abandoned dog. My mother was weeping fit to rend our hearts, while my father kept repeating hoarsely, 'That's enough! That'll do!' My brothers and I were terrified.

My older brother Viktor, who had just got married, had gone into hiding in a nearby town. The militia didn't manage to find him, and we set off for Siberia without him. But he was soon denounced by a 'well-intentioned' neighbour, who showed them the house where he had taken refuge. This cost him seven years' forced labour on the Bielomorkanal.[4] He'd initially been sentenced to three years, but as he'd tried to escape three times (he had the blood of the 'free Cossacks' in his veins!), he had his sentence extended by an extra three years. Once the six years had passed, he was told he was free. Before he left, he asked the boss a single question: 'Why was I sentenced to six years' forced labour?' The boss replied, 'So you still haven't realized why?' And, tearing up the papers that constituted Viktor's passport to freedom, he sent him back to the penal colony. A year later, when he was set free, my brother didn't ask any more questions. He took the papers certifying that he was free and left without a word.

Our great caravan of deportees, accompanied by the laments of the women and the squalling of the children, eventually arrived, after every kind of mishap, at the Pospelikha railway station. Here, a train formed of cattle trucks was waiting for us. We kids had never seen a train before, and we were filled with admiration for those fine wagons. But afterwards – what a let-down!

The wagon's heavy doors were kept closed, and it was forbidden to go out without the permission of the commandant accompanying the train. Light came in through the gaps and a tiny skylight. Once, someone opened the door to get a breath of air. He almost got himself killed by a soldier. We really were treated like criminals.

My parents improvised toilets in a corner of the wagon, with a big iron bucket hidden behind some blankets – rough-and-ready conveniences that you could use thanks to the darkness and the noise. But the most difficult thing to put up with was the suffocating atmosphere and the foul odour from the build-up of excrement. We were only officially allowed to empty the contents of the bucket during train stops, when the sliding door of the wagon was opened. But the men managed to empty it while the train was moving, and this made the air more breathable – it was already foetid because of the stove that kept the atmosphere constantly hot.

After a week of travelling, the convoy reached its destination, the Taiga station. It was a huge relief to be able to get out of the train. We were given provisional lodgings in some tumbledown huts, not far from the station. I'd fallen ill during the journey. A doctor came to listen to my chest. Since I didn't want to go any further, I tried to tamper with my thermometer, but unfortunately I shook it so hard that I broke it.

Two days later they handed out some food, and our long line of sleighs led by bearded men set out for the Bakchar region – none of us knew anything about it. Every time we asked a question, the guards would say, 'State secret'.

At daybreak, the guards divided us into groups of three families maximum, probably for security reasons. They must have been apprehensive that we might rebel if we were allowed to stay all together. Sorting out the groups took half a day. Nobody knew where we were being taken. When we finally set off, we tried to work out which direction we were headed by taking our bearings from the sun. Our direction was north-west. Very late that evening, we arrived outside the city of Tomsk.[5] Our route led around the city: eventually we reached a place surrounded by high fences, where there were three or four rudimentary huts.

One of the guards who had made friends with us told us we were being taken 180 kilometres from Tomsk. This was a valid way of measuring the distance in winter but in the summer it corresponded rather to a distance of 500 kilometres, since it wasn't possible to take a short cut through the marshes. They were quite impassable and you had to take a huge detour. The winter days were short, and we made only 40 kilometres per day. Our journey, either on foot or on horseback, lasted almost a week. Despite our hunger and the icy cold, we managed to reach the place we had been exiled to, Nizhne-Mokhovaya, safe and sound. As to how long we were going to live there, we hadn't the slightest idea. They told us it was for an indeterminate duration. Even today, certain deported families still live there; many of my classmates stayed there. As for me, after my second escape, which I'll return to later, I never went back.

Nizhne-Mokhovaya wasn't a strictly guarded zone. The administration merely requested the heads of families to report in regularly to the militia.

It was only in 1936 that Stalin's new Constitution authorized all the deportees to recover their civic rights – so they could, among other things, take part in electing deputies. But these new arrangements remained to some extent a dead letter. The local militia informed us that we no longer had the right to call each other 'comrades', and in particular we could not call *them* comrades. 'You need to forget the way everything used to be. From now on, your comrade is the wolf in the forests. We are your "head citizens". Just remember that!'

We were allotted room in a house where there was already a family of Old Believers, 'Kirzhaks',[6] who viewed us with some hostility. This was easy to understand: we were poor strangers, with five kids. They were worried we might ransack their vegetable garden.

But their fears were unfounded. Our father had sternly explained to us that we should serve as an example to everybody. Soon the word 'deportee' was replaced by the word 'special colonist'.

The youngsters were starting to go to school, which had just been organized. When spring arrived we had to get ready to work out in the fields. We had to sow some kind of crop. The main tools we had just then were axes, saws and buckets. We had to stub up the stumps of trees from a forest clearing, sow the grain by hand and cover it with earth. It was hellish work. And the swarms of mosquitoes and midges didn't make our task any easier. Even the mosquito nets we put over our heads didn't manage to protect us.

Everyone, without exception, worked in the fields, from the youngest kid who'd barely started to walk, to the oldest amongst us. In such inhuman conditions, we had to struggle to survive.

It's self-evident that to sow wheat or plant vegetables you need seeds. But how could we lay our hands on any? We had the idea of swapping all the clothes and various objects we could do without in exchange for these precious grains.

A peasant always counts on a good harvest. He lives in that hope. Succeeding in this task, at any cost, was a question of life or death for us.

I clearly remember the day when I was cutting barley with a sickle and I unfortunately slashed a finger on my left hand. They sprinkled a bit of ash from a hand-rolled cigarette over the wound, and that was that. I'll never forget what harsh times those were.

At the end of 1930, we were just starting to breathe again when disaster struck our family. Worn out by sorrow, labour and privations, my father died, exhausted. He wasn't even 48.

He had always forced himself to serve as an example to us. 'Don't be frightened of getting your hands dirty', he was always saying. 'Black hands can rake in a nice white kopek.' In other words, your hard work will eventually pay off. He had so longed for us to get that white kopek! 'He's killed himself working', my mother sobbed: she was utterly devastated by this cruel blow. Now she was all alone in a desolate region, surrounded by hostile people. And with five boys to feed.

That year, the winter was particularly cold. My father's death agony had taken place during a snowstorm. After his death, the storm blew up so violently that it was impossible for us to leave the house. And we had to keep our father's body in the house for a whole week, in a room that was even more freezing cold than the others. One day, shivering with cold, I went to the room where he was laid out; I cocked my ear and it seemed to me that I was going to hear him singing. Alas no, he wasn't singing 'Holy Lake Baikal', that song I loved so much, in which the Cossack rode up hill and down dale. It was just the snowstorm swirling round our house and threatening to tear off the roof of birch bark. I stayed with my father for so long that my mother was alarmed: she came looking for me and said, 'Your tears have turned into icicles.'

The storm dropped. The horse, which sank into the snow up to its nostrils, found it difficult to pull the sleigh. We had to put the coffin on huntsman's skis to take it to the cemetery. We dragged it along, stumbling through the snow, while the tears froze on our cheeks. Ivan, the oldest, was 16, Andrei was 14, I was 11, Vasili 10 and Nikolai 4.

With our father gone, the house seemed empty. How could we live without that man who could do everything, but hadn't had time to teach it to us?

I went back to school. To continue my studies, I had to go to the next village, fifteen kilometres away, and stay there all week. In winter, when the weather was fine, it was a pleasure to undertake this journey. But in the spring and autumn, it was quite a different matter. So as not to fall into the marshes, we had to walk across logs, keeping our balance while shooing off the swarms of midges and mosquitoes that came buzzing round us relentlessly.

Later on, during my military service, I went to the circus. A tightrope walker made a botch of his number, and I said to myself that he hadn't lived in Nizhne-Mokhovaya. I could have given him lessons myself!

At the school in Voronikha, the teachers, all deportees like us, were very competent. They did their best to give us an education. Nowadays I regret I didn't thank them for their dedication. Alas, it's too late now . . .

They had a difficult task on their hands: their pupils were all of different origins, and didn't have textbooks, exercise-books or even the least scrap of paper. We used to make our own exercise books ourselves, from birch-tree bark. These exercise books soon got stained with the blood of squashed mosquitoes.

Even the textbooks were made from birch bark. Necessity is the mother of invention.

A few years went by, and my mother decided to marry our neighbour, who already had three children: two daughters and one son. He was of Ukrainian nationality – a kind, hard-working fellow. His appearance in our home wasn't the kind of thing that met with my approval. I sometimes found myself concocting schemes to murder him. Every evening, I'd place an axe beneath my pillow. One morning, I finally decided to put my plans into action, but luckily, he'd already gone! Soon his kindness and patience finally won us over. With him, we started to build a new log izba, sawing down beams for the roof and the ceiling. My stepfather didn't draw any distinction between his own children and us: this made for a very united family.

FAREWELL TO SIBERIA

I was haunted by an intense homesickness for my village.

This life couldn't continue, and in 1934 the idea of going back to my home village to live with my sisters occurred to me. I thought things would better there.

My mother and my stepfather didn't want to let me go, but they soon realized they were wasting their breath. They prepared everything I might need on the journey. My stepfather gave me a wealth of advice, then pushed into my pocket a sheet of paper with a rudimentary plan of the route I would need to follow.

One hot summer's day, I gave everyone a hug and set out on the long journey to Kurya. I would have to cross the taiga and the steppes.

To begin with, I met with good luck. I met boys my own age. I would strike up a conversation with them, and in order to win their trust I used to improvise poetry and recite it to them – things like:

Petya's job is really hard,
They've given him the cows to guard.

One of the boys retorted that his name wasn't Petya, but
Ivan. Never mind: I just replaced 'Petya' by 'Ivan'. That
produced:

Ivan's job is really hard,
They've given him the cows to guard.
They're waiting for Ivan to doze off
And then they'll slip away fast enough!

This amused them, and they eventually invited me into their
homes, where this 'literary evening' continued. It all
reminded me of the good old days! Then they gave me
something to eat and a place for the night. Where did this
trust come from? Nowadays, nobody would ever let a
stranger into their homes.

I was still very credulous at that time. Five or six days after
I left, I met a middle-aged man on the road, with a knapsack
and a big stick in his hand. He became my travelling companion, and told me all sorts of stories. I thought he was perfectly sincere, and took him for a decent bloke.

It was a Saturday evening. As we were coming into a village, I suggested we spend the night in a peasants' house, as
I'd been doing up until now. He categorically refused – his
excuse was that we might be caught by the militia and sent to
jail. So he suggested we ate what we still had, and he headed
off to the village to suss things out. After waiting for quite a
while, when I'd started to think he'd never come back, he did
return and told me he'd found a safe place – an abandoned
shed in a farmyard. I had no desire to spend the night there
without the permission of its owners, but I couldn't persuade
him. We went to sleep. The next morning, both my

knapsack and my travelling companion had vanished. I didn't know what to do.

The householder found me in floods of tears and asked me what I was doing near his shed. I told him everything: he felt sorry for me, and invited me into his home. They gave me a meal, shaking their heads over how naive I'd been. They even gave me food for my journey.

It wasn't long before I'd eaten all my provisions, and I still had a good deal of the route to travel. Pangs of hunger were gnawing at me more and more. What should I do? Stealing was out of the question. I remembered the beggars who used to come for alms in Kurya, and how mother had warned us that we should never look them in the eye. If they didn't look you in the eye, it was okay, she said. But I would still have had to find the right words to make people feel sorry for me. I couldn't. I preferred to starve.

I had the impression that the villages on my route were getting poorer and poorer, and the people who lived in them less and less inclined to charity. I never managed to hold out my hand and utter the appropriate words. One day, an elderly woman with a kindly face came up to me and gently said, 'Listen, sonny, stealing is a shameful sin, but there's nothing wrong with holding your hand out. God is merciful. You simply need to conquer your pride!'

Later on, I tried to understand why she hadn't given me alms herself. Even today, I still sometimes think of that mysterious babushka. That kindly face, that gentle gaze, that stirring voice – she had saved my life. I've forgotten the words I uttered as I held my hand out. The only thing that remains engraved in my memory is that, before I swallowed my bread, I swallowed my tears – and these seemed much harder to swallow than the bread.

Only after a week did I reach the rail station at Taiga, where I hid in a goods train en route for Pospelikha. From here I had to travel another 65 kilometres on foot to reach Kurya.

Late in the evening, I knocked on the door of my sister Niura, who lived in a village very close to Kurya. When she saw me, she couldn't believe her eyes. She kept saying, 'Is it really you, Misha?' It seemed incredible to her that I could have made that long and difficult journey all by myself. She plied me with endless questions: how was mother, how were her brothers, how was stepfather? I patiently answered her questions.

I absolutely didn't want to sponge off my sister. After resting for two weeks, it was time to look for work. I was too young for heavy peasant labour, but I could help with cutting the branches off the trees before they were felled. So I spent a few days at the home of my brother Viktor's wife. One day, before going off to work, I accidentally left on the table a letter I was going to send to my brother. I told him about his child, born after he'd left – the child seemed to suffer from abnormalities. My sister-in-law came across the letter and sent me packing without further ado. I didn't feel any sense of guilt: I'd simply told the truth.

In fact, I didn't feel at home anywhere in Kurya. Neither at my sisters' nor anywhere else.

So I decided to go back to Siberia. I had a lot of friends there; and I really ought to carry on with my studies. Before I left, I decided to have one last look round the place where our house had been. It had been burnt down. There was nothing left, and I had to make an effort to reconstruct the past in my memory. The neighbours who saw me said to my sister Gasha afterwards: 'Misha was looking for something on the site of your house – he must have been after gold!' My sister replied that after we'd gone she had wanted to dig up the remaining potatoes, but there was nothing left; even the basement had been demolished. What gold could they have meant?

Standing in front of the ashes of our house I wasn't thinking of gold, but I did remember the lines by Sergei Esenin that we'd copied onto birch bark at Voronikha:

> *Here I'm known to nobody,*
> *Even my friends have forgotten me.*
> *And where my house could once be found,*
> *The ashes now swirl all around.*

For me at the time, this poetry was worth more than gold – and it still is.

So I was on my travels again. I reached Pospelikha in a lorry, then I got to the station at Taiga without any problems. But this time, the journey I'd made on foot three months earlier turned out to be much more difficult. I drank the water from the streams. On the second day I felt a sharp pain in my stomach. It was impossible to continue with my journey. I just managed to struggle as far as the nearest house, lay down near the entry and went to sleep. When I opened my eyes, I saw two old women. When they learned what had happened to me, they brought me a potion that tasted absolutely foul – I can still remember it. That evening I drank some more, and I also took a little gruel and a cup of tea. I spent the night comfortably in a hay barn. The next morning, after another dose of the potion and another cup of tea, I went on my way.

My illness had left me feeling debilitated, and I had to keep stopping to draw breath. It was still daylight when I reached Nizhne-Mokhovaya. But crossing the village, where everyone knew me, was out of the question given the state I was in. I lit a fire and started to wait for dusk. The day dragged on. I was attacked by swarms of mosquitoes that weren't afraid of the smoke from my fire. Eventually night fell and I crossed the threshold of my house.

Mother gave me something to eat and she in turn asked me lots of questions about her daughters and about her son Viktor. Then I went up into the loft, where there was a bed and mosquito net. Here we chatted with my brothers until daybreak.

This was the end of my first journey. How many kilometres had I covered, and what was the point of battling through all those difficulties?

I continued my studies at the school in Voronikha. I told myself that I hadn't planned my first journey properly and that I was still too young. I needed to wait until I came of age before applying for a passport – and my request would probably be turned down. But I absolutely needed one. What should I do? This problem occupied my thoughts night and day. Finally I decided to go back to Kurya, but this time with a document that would enable me to obtain a passport. This indispensable document was to be signed not by the village council, but by the regional administration and drawn up on a special form with the stamp and seal of the state.

I decided to engrave the seals myself. In the loft I had a workshop where I made containers of beech-bark, since there wasn't much in the way of kitchen implements and we didn't have enough money to buy any. Here I could lock myself away and continue with my experiments.

I became very taciturn. My behaviour worried my mother, who would have liked to have known what was on my mind, why I was disappearing more and more often, and for longer and longer periods in my workshop – where I eventually obtained some satisfactory results.

To carry out my plan, I needed an accomplice, someone I could rely on. My pal Gavril Bondarenko, a couple of years older than me, shared my dreams of escape. He worked as an accountant in the kolkhoz office. He often used to ask

me to give him a hand in the office, and I was only too glad
to help out. This time I was the one who asked him to give
me a non-registered document with the stamp and seal of
the administration. So one fine day he brought me just
what I needed, though he pointed out that the document
would absolutely need to be returned. 'Of course', I replied,
and asked him to give me a few sheets of paper as well.
Clutching this treasure to my chest, I climbed up into my
workshop.

It took me days to reproduce the official stamp and seal.
When I showed the results of my labours to Gavril, he didn't
believe me and asked me where I'd got those forms – the
fakes seemed so authentic! This was my first invention, and
my first step towards freedom!

With these papers, I could return to my home village,
obtain a passport and get a job. But to fulfil this dream I
needed money – so what about selling papers like this as a
way of making money? Every deportee dreamed of returning
to his or her home village.

We went into a village where nobody knew us. Gavril,
who had neat handwriting, filled out the forms that we then
sold to the deportees. In this way we made a bit of money,
and we could think about setting off.

This time our parents realized that their efforts to dis-
suade us were in vain. My mother was anxious. She kept
saying, 'You suffered so much during your first journey,
Misha!' I retorted, 'It's freedom we're after. So you mustn't
cry.' But she was still crying when she replied, 'Everyone
knows what that freedom of yours is worth!'

One fine morning in 1936, taking every precaution, we left
the village. Passing by the cemetery, I suggested to my
companion that we go and visit my father's tomb. 'Of course',
he said. 'I knew him well.' It took us a while, looking among
all the weeds before we found a wooden cross with his name

half worn away. We stood there for a while in silence and then I said, with tears in my eyes, 'Forgive me, Father! I'm going away to seek freedom. Wish me good luck!'

Still in silence, we set off. Suddenly a hare broke out of the undergrowth. He looked just as if he was making fun of us, as we walked along with our gun. We were amused to see that intrepid hare dashing down the road ahead of us, and then scampering off to the side. Why did he scamper off so suddenly? A hundred meters further on, we spotted the traces of a fox. That explained everything. Animals are cautious; it's the only way they can stay safe and sound. We needed to follow this excellent example and act with circumspection.

A few kilometres further on, we saw the first village. As we crossed it, I walked ahead, pretending to be some malefactor en route to jail. Gavril followed me, holding his rifle. He was the escort.

Coming out of the village, we jumped into the bushes, laughing our heads off. We kept saying, 'It worked!' And we decided to have a bite to eat – some cooked potatoes (still warm), sauerkraut, cucumber, bread and pancakes. Since she knew I liked pancakes, Mother had made a great number of them for me and put them in a birch-wood container – this was the last piece of kitchen equipment I ever constructed, but also the most handsome.

Before leaving, we had impressed on our families that nobody should be told about our departure. We bought an old cheap rifle especially so we could act out our roles as 'prisoner and escort' and thus get through the villages without too many risks. When they saw us, the women would exclaim, 'He's a young lad to have strayed from the straight and narrow! Whatever is the world coming to?' This game gave us a great deal of amusement. But one day, as we were passing in front of the local administration offices, some horsemen who were arguing fiercely nodded to Gavril and shouted, 'Keep a close eye on that bandit!' We started walking more quickly. Then we heard the order, 'Check their papers!' We just had time to hide in the thick forest. As we waited for night to fall, we sheltered among the trees. The next day, we decided to get rid of the rifle. So we chucked it in the river, even though it had saved us several times over – before almost betraying us.

On the fifth day we reached the village where Gavril's family lived. 'We'd never have recognized you!' his aunts exclaimed tearfully. 'You've grown so much!' Once again, a host of questions: 'How is everybody? And your little brother?' Gavril told them everything in the greatest detail, and I listened attentively. Once again it was the story of a family of deportees.

The next morning, Gavril went to the militia to get his passport. I was terribly worried. When he came back to the house, he rushed in at top speed and announced, 'I'm getting my passport tomorrow!' I could have wept for joy – but I immediately started wondering, 'Why tomorrow? Why not today? Perhaps they want to double-check?'

We couldn't sleep that night, and kept mulling over all eventualities. But Gavril soon received his temporary passport, and we set off for my home village. Shortly after, I in turn obtained my temporary passport.

At Kurya, we got work at the agricultural machinery centre – Gavril as an accountant, and myself as a supervisor. But shortly after, we were obliged to leave the village, due to an almost surrealist episode that changed my destiny.

On the return journey from Siberia to Kurya, we had passed through Gavril's village, where we'd picked up a pistol that he kept hidden away at home. Then, when we arrived in my village, at my sister Niura's where we planned to live for a while, I'd hidden the pistol in her cellar. Alas, someone denounced us to the militia, either because we'd been spotted hiding it, or because we'd been bragging about it to the other lads. As a result I got myself arrested. It was just before the New Year. I spent three or four days at the local militia station, where I was interrogated harshly, but I remained inflexible. I didn't want to admit that we had a firearm. I kept trying to find some way of escape. The window to the toilets seemed one possible escape route. I was released for the holiday: they hoped I understood the gravity of my offence, and that I'd hand the weapon in straight after the start of the New Year. But I'd decided to keep the pistol at any cost. I was drawn to it – we'd become inseparable. My friend and I realized that this might cause us more than one headache. It was then that we decided to leave. I'd made up my mind not to hand in that weapon, but I realized they'd never leave us alone. So we decided to do a bunk.

I think it was dating from this episode, and thanks to that pistol, that my passion for weapons started.

I sometimes say that it was because of the Germans that I became a weapons designer. In fact, that's not entirely true. Long before the war, I was as attached to that pistol as if it was my brother! I wanted to find out how it was made, and understand its mechanisms. I was forever taking it to pieces and putting it back together again, polishing every piece and carefully oiling it. We even had some ammunition, and we indulged in some shooting practice. When we decided to leave the village, we took the pistol apart and scattered the pieces here, there, and everywhere through the forests along our route, so no one would be able to reassemble them. I did so with a heavy heart and tears in my eyes. Why did we do this? Actually, we were damn scared of being caught by the militia in possession of this implement. It was strictly forbidden to possess a personal weapon.

Gavril and I had decided to head for Kazakhstan, where his brother worked on the railways. We'd sent him a letter, and he wrote to tell us that he'd find us work.

When we got there, we stayed in the sleeping wagons of the rail depot, which suited us down to the ground! I was a member of the Komsomol, the Communist youth organization. One day, I was summoned to the political department at the depot. To begin with I panicked, but eventually I found they just wanted to offer me a job as a technical secretary, since I had neat handwriting. I did this job for two years: it consisted mainly of answering the telephone and filling in forms. But I was haunted by the fear that someone might learn about my past as a deportee.

*   *   *

I have often been tempted to relate these episodes from my youth, and each time I abandoned the idea. Could I safely reveal this part of my existence? My destiny might have been quite different, since people could have decided that the author of these revelations had no right to work in such a secret field as the weapons industry.

Astonishing as it might seem, nobody among my closest relatives, children and grandchildren included, ever knew anything about this period in my life. I don't like Gorbachev, but I have to admit that perestroika made it possible for me to bring this whole hidden tragic side of my life out into the open. I was able to look my past in the face and speak to people about it without being afraid I might be denounced.

Today, I thank destiny for having enabled me to serve my country, which I have always loved, even in the bitterest periods that it has endured.

2

'ARISE, GREAT COUNTRY! ARISE TO MORTAL FIGHT!'[1]

When the young Kalashnikov was called up, the Soviet Army was still called the 'RKKA' (the Russian initials of the name 'Red Army of Workers and Peasants'). Organized in 1918 by Lenin and more particularly by Trotsky (whose name disappeared completely from history textbooks at the end of the 1920s, and even today is hardly ever mentioned), it kept this name until 1946.

Initially made up of volunteers backed by the Party, it became obligatory four months after its creation, and remained so. Even today, young Russians are forced to serve two years in the army once they reach the age of 18.

Shortly before 1938, the year in which Kalashnikov joined the army, 800 superior officers, including Marshal Tukhachevsky, were arrested, and many of them were shot. This was part of a thoroughgoing 'renovation' of the Soviet High Command. Contrary to received ideas about the weakness of the USSR's military potential, it was, in certain branches, superior to that of Germany. The famous T34 tanks, *for instance, were more advanced and better equipped than those of their future enemies. On the other hand, the army was short of individual weapons and ammunition. Marshal Zhukov relates in his Memoirs, 'Incredible as it may sound, we had to beg for ammunition. Our orders were to consume a maximum of two cartridges every 24 hours, even in heavy fighting.'*

On the eve of the war, the armed forces, commanded by Stalin in person, numbered five million soldiers. When war against Nazi Germany broke out, in June 1941, the lack of senior officers was felt as a severe handicap, which partly explains the Soviet defeats. The German High Command, predicting a Blitzkrieg, launched a military operation named 'typhoon', the plan for the drive towards and invasion of Moscow in late 1941.

It was during this battle that Sergeant Kalashnikov was wounded while commanding a tank, and became trapped in the German encirclement. The opening of the Bryansk front slowed down the advance of the Reich's forces on Moscow, but the German communiqué boasted of having captured 630,000 prisoners. By an amazing stroke of luck, Kalashnikov, though severely wounded, managed to escape and ended up in a military hospital in October 1941.

At the start of this year, Zhukov had been appointed commander of the forces on the western front. From August 1942 onwards, he became the sole adjutant of the Commander-in-Chief. Stalin, probably aware of his own incompetence, no longer took any decisions without consulting him. In autumn 1942, General Zhukov (he was appointed Marshal in 1943) devised the plan to capture the Germans in a pincer movement in the Stalingrad region: he emerged victorious from this decisive phase of the war.

Throughout these years, Kalashnikov was working behind the front lines on the prototypes of different firearms, especially the future AK-47, which was to become famous. The organization of the area behind the front lines played a major role in ensuring victory, and the different republics in the east of the Soviet Union provided irreplaceable support. More than 2,500 industrial operations, and half of all engineers, were evacuated here. The production of arms industries needed to make up for the material losses sustained at the front. The whole population was mobilized: women, retired people and children all worked in shifts, 24 hours a day. Gulag prisoners (scientists, engineers, technicians, designers) were kept busy behind barbed wire contributing to the victory of the Soviet Union. Several imprisoned officers were released and joined their units with the grades they had had before their arrest. A special foundation for the defence of the country took gifts from citizens: a portion of their salaries was paid into it on a voluntary basis. Nothing was too fine or beautiful to be sacrificed for victory: people gave up their most precious belongings.

Kalashnikov, meanwhile, worked on tirelessly, hoping that his weapon would be used for the defence of his native land.

THE LAST BUT ONE

In autumn 1938, I was called up in the town of Stryi, in western Ukraine. The Soviet Army was at that time called the 'Red Army of Workers and Peasants'.

When I reached the conscripts' base, I presented myself to the man in charge and told him of my passion for mechanical things, and my competence in handling them. At school in Siberia, I'd had a fantastic physics professor who really encouraged me in my studies. One day, to his intense amazement, I'd brought him a perpetual (or almost perpetual) motion machine. It seemed to me that I was only a whisker away from total success!

I was assigned to the company that trained mechanics to drive tanks. We'd taken courses in military technology and other disciplines. The NCOs paid particular attention to the cleanliness of our uniforms, our discipline and the way we marched. Because I was on the short side, I always occupied the last but one place when we were marching. It was obvious that the sergeant-major didn't like me very much. He kept making digs at my expense; he gave me the nickname 'last but one', and he was always nit-picking. This provoked me into feelings of rebelliousness, which often ended up with my being given extra chores to do: I had to clean the barracks floor, make and remake my bed countless times, wash the toilet block and march all by myself up and down the deserted yard.

From time to time, I was given completely absurd tasks to do. My sergeant-major was very inventive in this area. But this didn't stop me standing up to him.

On the wall of our barracks they used to stick up a sort of weekly newspaper devoted to life in our company. My sergeant-major suggested to the editor-in-chief of this news poster that they hold a competition to find out who could do the best drawing of me, the 'last but one', marching all by myself in the yard. When I heard about this, I composed a very funny poem about myself and my 'failings'. The lads in the editorial department liked my poem so much that they put it beneath my caricature. That evening my superior officer himself read out the poem in a sarcastic tone of voice, and aroused general hilarity. After which, he told me, 'You see, you couldn't fall much lower, my boy – everyone has to take a hand in helping you know what's what.' The lads who knew that I was the one who'd written the poem gave each other a knowing wink. The next day, everyone knew who'd written the poem. This came as quite a surprise to my superior officer, especially as he himself had praised my little piece. Finally, he gave me a position on the editorial board of the newspaper, and my reputation as a poet continued to soar. Shortly after, my poems started to appear in the army newspapers, and my sergeant-major himself became extremely proud of me. He even tried to change my place in the ranks! Thanks to him I took part in the congress of 'young writers' in the army at Kiev. But some criticisms of my poems were voiced: 'Why do you only ever talk about tanks, bullets, shells and the other weapons of war? Why not sing of our leaders who are working with such dedication for the glory of our country?'

During my military service, I learnt everything to do with tanks, including driving them and shooting from them, both in theory and in practice. At that period, tank servers were equipped with TT pistols – 'TT' means 'Tulka-Tokarev', i.e. 'Tokarev model, from the town of Tula'.[2] This weapon wasn't in the least bit easy to fire. It wasn't a bad pistol in itself, but it wasn't very well adapted for tank combat. Firing out in the open and firing from inside a tank through a narrow loophole are two completely different things. The experience I'd acquired during the episode of the hidden pistol served me well. I managed to suggest an improvement that made it easier to shoot through the loophole. This time I didn't have to keep my interests secret – we had experimental workshops placed at our disposal.

In May 1940, General Zhukov was given command of the army in the Kiev region.[3] He encouraged his soldiers to be creative. Every week, a technical problem was submitted to the conscripts, who had to try and solve it. On one occasion, a competition was set up to invent a piece of apparatus that could keep count of the number of times a tank had fired. I knuckled down to it and got some very good results. To begin with, they ribbed me a bit, calling me the 'local

Edison'. But our chiefs saw that it worked, and they started to look at me rather differently.

An article about me came out in the army newspaper. This was the first time my talents as an inventor had been officially recognized. The experts described my invention as 'easy to make and reliable'. Even now, I'm still grateful to my commander for having supported me in my efforts.

On another occasion, we were asked to devise an apparatus that would measure how well a tank engine was functioning. The practical importance of such an apparatus for tank crews was obvious. After several months of work, I tried out a prototype on my own tank; it worked perfectly. My chiefs decided to send it to the military authorities in Kiev, and me with it. I was only supposed to stay there for three days, but in the end I never went back to my barracks! The military experts tested out my apparatus, and wrote a report to General Zhukov himself: he immediately sent for me.

Zhukov greeted me in a warm, simple manner, and tried to put me at my ease, but I have to admit I was feeling pretty nervous. When I went into his office, there were other military personnel there, including several generals. I'll never forget this meeting. Zhukov spoke to me very simply, and didn't beat about the bush. He said, 'Listen, it's really excellent that someone like you, an ordinary soldier, can set a good example. It's not just scientists and weapons engineers, but ordinary soldiers too who should be thinking of ways to improve our equipment. We ought to send you to Moscow; but you do actually need to have another look at the external appearance of your invention, it looks too amateurish. You ought to work on it in Kiev, to start off with. We've got a technical school for tanks there, with good workshops.'

As this was a ukase (an edict or decree) from the general, they helped me to make two very fine pieces of equipment. And I was called in to see Zhukov for a second time, to show him these two brand-new, shiny black gadgets. He seemed very pleased with the result, and he congratulated me. In reward for my work, he gave me a beautiful watch, which I unfortunately lost later on. This meeting was a turning-point in my destiny.

Zhukov ordered me to go to Moscow. At Kubinka, not far from the capital, they organized some trials. But we arrived there too late: the competition was already over. It was a colonel's invention that had passed the trials most brilliantly, and been chosen for mass production. However, Zhukov wasn't just anybody: since he'd asked them to test my apparatus, the organizers did so, reluctantly. By the end of the trials, they'd realized that my meter was clearly the more efficient! So this was the one recommended for mass production.

In spring 1941, I was sent to Leningrad to launch the production of this model. I was only 22, but the chief engineer at the factory greeted me as his equal. During my time here, I realized how much patience and collective effort was necessary for the mass production of each piece. It was teamwork between engineers, workers and technicians. On 22 June, war against Nazi Germany broke out, and turned our plans upside-down. The project was far from completion, but I had to rejoin my regiment. 'We won't be separated for long. Once we've won the war, we'll carry on with this work', the factory manager told me in farewell.

At the time, everyone thought the war would unfold in accordance with Soviet military doctrine: the minimum of losses, stopping the enemy at the borders – Stalin and Hitler had made a non-aggression pact in 1939. But there was a sense of danger in the air. The war was raging in other parts of Europe. We weren't at all prepared. The soldiers hadn't been given the necessary training. We'd hardly learned how to shoot. The Germans were far more experienced. In addition to their training, they'd already experienced war in other countries: they were a formidable foe. The slogans of the time said, 'We we will not yield an inch of our land.' But the Germans made a quick break-through – it was spectacular. In addition, we'd only just annexed a new territory, West Ukraine. Not everyone there was on our side. Hitler's troops advanced without meeting any real resistance.

During the first days of the war, during the battle of Bryansk, I had the fright of my life. My lieutenant had ordered me to climb up a tree to observe the enemy. He thought the Germans were a long way from our positions. I happily shinned up the tree and was horrified to discover that the Germans were really close. The minute they saw me, they started taking pot-shots at me. Bullets whistled past my ears. That day, I got down the tree in record time. A squirrel couldn't have done it any quicker!

The bombardments were also pretty terrifying. Luckily I was a tank server: in a tank, you feel incomparably safer than you do out in the open.

Most of the soldiers in our company were very young. Our lieutenant was the highest-ranking officer. Without experience or equipment, we were at a loss when faced with the enemy. I remember the battle of Bryansk as if it were yesterday: on mountainous, heavily forested terrain there were scenes of indescribable confusion. During these first days of the conflict, we had very few weapons. Some of us only had flame-throwers, which couldn't be used more than two or three times. No rifles or sub-machine guns. In fact, we were cannon-fodder. I really regretted not having received any training worthy of the name. The Germans were armed to the teeth!

At the start of the war, I had been trained as a tank driver and mechanic. But eventually I found myself in charge of the vehicle, even though I didn't have any real experience.

The battle lasted several days. We thought the earth was burning up all around us. The orders we had received were: 'Don't shoot or else you'll give away your positions.' The Messerschmitts were flying in low to reconnoitre, and could easily discover our whereabouts. Shortly afterwards, we were bombed. Still, we continued to obey orders: 'Don't shoot!' This happened several times.

On one occasion, several tanks got left behind. There was firing on all sides. Suddenly, everything seemed to go quiet. As tank commander, I decided to open the turret hatch to see what was happening in the vicinity. And just then, a shell exploded right near me. Pieces of shrapnel went right through my chest and back. I didn't feel anything at the time. And when I saw the bloodstains on the tank, I wondered which of my men had got wounded. Then my head started to spin, and I lost consciousness. Even now I still get pains which make it difficult for me to write.

When I came round, my company was no longer on the battlefield. My arm and my left shoulder seemed to belong to somebody else. My back was hurting appallingly. My left arm was completely immobile. I was lucky: I could easily have lost it. There was complete chaos all around me. For two days I stayed in a bunker that my comrades took me to. When the army doctor arrived, he gave me a thorough checking over. Then he declared: 'Contusion. He needs to be taken to hospital.'

But how were we to get there? It was a real problem, since we were surrounded by the German armies. They assembled twelve wounded men, and put them in an ambulance. A doctor and a nurse accompanied us. I can still remember the name of the driver: Kolya. All our hopes rested on him: most of us were unable to walk.

Night was falling by the time we came to a village, and the doctor gave the order to stop here. We had to find out if there were any German soldiers about. Some scouts were picked: the driver Kolya, a lieutenant who'd got burns on his arms, and myself. All those who could walk, in fact. The only weapons we had were a pistol and a rifle. Everything was quiet, the village seemed dead. Suddenly, we heard bursts of gunfire from automatic weapons. We flung ourselves to the ground and tried to get back to the forest, across a potato field. When we were near the ambulance, we heard more gunfire. The lieutenant whispered, 'they're shooting with Schmeissers.[4] If only we had a sub-machine gun of some description . . .' I gripped my TT pistol, and we ran to the car. When we arrived, Germans in a side-car were disappearing round the bend in the road. It was a terrible sight: all the wounded had been machine-gunned, and the streams of blood formed a puddle at the bottom of the car.

We kept running for as long as we could, trying to get as far away from the road as possible. We walked all night, making very slow and difficult progress. My shoulder was racked with pain. From time to time I lost consciousness. Poor Kolya dragged me along and helped me to walk. The lieutenant wasn't in any better shape than I was. The following day, Kolya spotted an elderly peasant carrying a little bag. We told him of our misfortune and asked for help. He told us the Germans had confiscated all their provisions, and forbidden them to gather any food from the fields. But he went there in secret as he had to feed his family. 'Okay, I'll take you to the village doctor; he lives 15 kilometres from here. He's a very kind chap.'

Three hundred metres from the village, he advised us to wait for nightfall, wished us good luck and left us there. We waited in a state of intense anxiety. We observed the scene in silence for a while, and realized that there wasn't any sound of activity. In fact the village seemed deserted. So Kolya went off to reconnoitre. Shortly afterwards he returned with a little satchel. When he opened it, we almost wept for joy: there was half a home-made loaf, two boiled potatoes, two apples and a little salt. Kolya told us that the doctor had given him something to eat at home, and this food was for us.

While we ate, he told us that the doctor had three sons at the front. The Germans had already been to his house and had even taken him twice to the Kommandantur (Military Headquarters). So he asked us to be especially careful, and to come only after nightfall.

The doctor received us in a room where all his medical instruments were laid out on a table. The windows were covered by sheets. He took off our dirty, bloodied bandages, cleaned our wounds and sores, and put on some clean dressings. He refused to let us leave, as our wounds were really dangerous. 'You absolutely need two or three days' bed rest. I can hide you in the barn, it's full of hay.' When I think of the insane risks he was taking! If the Germans had discovered us, they'd have strung him up.

So I found myself back in the hay that I had so loved in my childhood. I was filled with sad memories. I thought of my family. My brothers were probably at the front. My mother was all alone. Would I ever see her again? First, I would need to get out of this slaughter-house alive. The doctor gave us water, food and a number of journals and books, most of them medical. My memory, probably sharpened by my intense anxiety, has retained an incredible amount of medical information. Even now I can give an expert opinion to my friends whenever they go down with an illness. On the other hand, I feel guilty that I didn't ask for our saviour's surname. For us he was always Nikolai Ivanovich.

When we were more or less in a fit state to walk, Nikolai Ivanovich showed us in which direction the nearest front lines lay, and the safest path that led there. As before, we walked by night and rested up during the daytime, saving as much food as we could. Three days later, there was still no sight of the front, and less and less sight of our food. So we went over to a primitive diet: raw mushrooms, wild berries – we even munched grass. The only water you could find was in the swamps: this stagnant water gave us heartburn and stomach-ache.

All around us there was a strange, suspicious calm. It was as if, instead of getting closer to the front, we were actually getting further away. But we kept heading west, as indicated by the doctor. It was only after a whole week of wanderings and difficulties that we came face to face with our own soldiers again. This was near the town of Trubchevsk.

We gave ourselves up as prisoners of our own army, since we'd crossed German lines and weren't carrying any papers. Every Russian soldier's worst nightmare was to fall into German hands: we'd avoided the worst, and were safe. After a short interrogation, the lieutenant and I were sent to hospital, while Kolya reassumed his job as an army driver.

MY UNIVERSITY – THE HOSPITAL

In the hospital, a doctor gave me a good telling off. 'How could you have let your wound get so infected?' Of course he didn't know anything about my adventures or all the things I'd been through. He warned me that I was in for a long convalescence.

At night I was haunted by nightmares: I was running through the forest, trying to dodge the bursts of enemy machine-gun fire. I could see myself in the ambulance, lying among the wounded, and I'd wake up with a start. The people in the neighbouring beds were evidently also prey to bad dreams. Their groans stopped me getting back to sleep.

Day and night I was obsessed by one thought: how could such a debacle have occurred? After all, our chiefs had promised us that we'd fight with minimal losses and with the most up-to-date weapons. But all the wounded men around me kept saying the same thing: they could count themselves lucky if they had as much as one rifle between two. Fortunately, we outnumbered the enemy.

The lessons of the past had been wasted. The history of the Crimean War and the First World War was being repeated. My thoughts were simple and concrete: where were those light, efficient automatic weapons that we so desperately needed? I dreamt of only one thing: what if I could create my own automatic sub-machine gun? When I was a tank commander, I'd had occasion to use the Degtyarev sub-machine gun.[5] I'd taken it apart and reassembled it many times. This weapon was very widely used during the war against Finland, just before the Second World War. It was more efficient than any other weapon in close combat. It was light, easy to transport and could fire uninterruptedly: all of these qualities earned it its name of sub-machine gun. The famous weapons designer Federov[6] had written in 1939, in his book *The Development of Firearms*:

> The sub-machine gun is a relatively young weapon that made its appearance during the First World War. Even today, the fabulous future awaiting this weapon is still not fully appreciated. In time it will surely become an essential weapon, since it is powerful, light, and easy to build. It still needs to be improved. Sub-machine guns are irreplaceable in close combat, where there is no need for higher-calibre bullets.

General Federov showed considerable courage in publishing his reflections at that time. I was just an ordinary soldier, quite unaware of the struggle for power that was raging around the issue of the sub-machine gun in the upper echelons. Among the critics of this weapon there was a man who was very influential at the time, the adjutant of the People's Commissar (Minister) for Defence, Gennadi Kulik. Kulik was head of the Main Artillery Directorate. How could I, a mere wounded soldier, have known that, in February 1939, production of the Degtyarev sub-machine gun had quite simply been stopped, and the copies in circulation in the army had been withdrawn and put into storage? The consequence of this senseless act was that the Red Army was deprived of this essential weapon. In addition, it became impossible to study it or to learn its tactical characteristics, its qualities and particular features. The designers Federov, Degtyarev and Shpagin[7] were still fighting to rehabilitate the sub-machine gun in the army. They were doing everything they could to convince the government; Degtyarev in particular insisted that it needed to be modernized and mass-produced. They were following developments in foreign technology closely, and they were fully aware that completely automatic weapons, including sub-machine guns, were being used more and more in other armies, especially in the German army. The USSR had no right to fall behind.

The war against Finland, in 1939, had demonstrated the effectiveness of this weapon; it had been a powerful firearm on wooded, hilly terrain, especially in conditions of close combat. The Finns used Suomi sub-machine guns that caused havoc in our ranks, especially when used by their ski units.

At the end of 1939, the Supreme Military Council took the decision to continue mass production of the Degtyarev sub-machine gun. It was only on 6 January 1940 that the Defence Committee decided to place it at the disposal of the army. Degtyarev improved his weapon so as to reduce the time it took to manufacture: it became simpler and more lightweight.

Several designers poured into the breach and started working on prototypes of an automatic weapon. From among the designers, the highly talented Shpagin emerged the winner. He was the first to get the idea of stamping the pieces under heat. He writes in his *Memoirs*: 'Even the great specialists in arms manufacture did not believe it was possible to create such an automatic weapon. But I was convinced of the correctness of my reasoning.'

When we met, after the war, Georgi Shpagin told me that the competition with other designers had been fierce. He worked for only six months on his prototype and, on 21 December 1940, the Defence Committee took the decision to issue the Red Army with his sub-machine gun. But this was put into service only a few months before Russia's entry into the Second World War. This is why, during the first battles, the Red Army felt the lack of this weapon so badly.

In 1941, during what were doubtless the darkest hours of the war, Voronov[8] was appointed head of the Red Army artillery. But he was also in charge of more lightweight firearms. Stalin himself oversaw the distribution of sub-machine guns and anti-tank rifles. And this is what Marshal Voronov wrote in his *Memoirs*, in 1963:

The year 1942 was approaching. On the evening of 31 December, I was called to general staff headquarters, where I was informed that two battalions of skiers were to be sent to the front. They were not armed with any assault weapons, and they needed to be equipped as a matter of urgency. After several investigations, I realized that I had only 250 assault rifles: this was what our reserves of firearms had come down to. I reported this information to general staff. I was told to supply the two battalions of skiers with 160 assault rifles and to keep the rest in reserve. This was how we celebrated the New Year of 1942. Although our possibilities were very limited, we firmly believed that victory would be ours.

But as I lay there on my hospital bed, I couldn't know any of this.

At that time I thought that Degtyarev was the only designer able to create a reliable, light, small-calibre sub-machine gun. However, it seemed to me that his model was far from perfect. And at night, I started to dream of devising a weapon that would be far superior to it. During the day, I spent my time sketching out what I had imagined during the night, in a notebook I'd managed to get hold of. This idea completely obsessed me. It was starting to make me ill. I went over my drawings countless times each day. But my lack of know-how was obvious, and this caused me terrible frustration.

When I'd devised my metre to count the number of times a tank was fired, the knowledge I'd acquired at school and in the army had been sufficient. My natural intuition, com-bined with my experience, had enabled me to design that particular piece of apparatus. On the other hand, I was com-pletely lacking in any expertise when it came to designing a revolutionary weapon. I was aware of the enormity of the obstacle. Despite the intense, nagging pain in my shoulder, I went to the hospital library every day: it was a particularly valuable resource for me. Here I found several books that had a decisive impact on my life, including Federov's two volumes on *The Evolution of Firearms*.

In the huge hospital ward where my bed was, I was sur-rounded by members of tank crews, artillerymen, infantrymen and mine clearance experts. We'd often talk about the advan-tages and disadvantages of different types of weapon. I listened attentively to the remarks of those who had used sub-machine guns in combat. This gave me ideas for my own designs and research. I'd drawn up a table on which I'd written the differ-ent types of automatic weapons, the history of their design, and then their technical and tactical characteristics, which I attempted to compare. A lieutenant in the parachutists, who had worked before the war as a scientist in a research institute, gave me a considerable amount of help in understanding the mechanisms involved in automatic weapons. It was a huge piece of good luck for me to have this man there to help me. It was he, together with the two volumes of Federov (which I read and reread from A to Z), who enabled me to make progress in my research.

One day, the lieutenant explained to me the meaning of the word 'automatic' in Greek: 'that which works all by itself'. This means, in the case of a weapon, that when you press on a trigger, it fires without stopping. That's the main merit of the sub-machine gun. The lieutenant shared my opinion on the future of rapid-fire automatic weapons. He was convinced that the sub-machine guns of Shpagin and Degtyarev were superior to their German equivalents. He had had an opportunity to use the Finnish Suomi M-31 too, and the German MP-38, which we called – I have no idea why – the 'Schmeisser', even though the inventor of that name was unconnected to the MP-38. All our soldiers found that the Russian sub-machine guns were lighter and more effective than the enemy's, and wondered why we didn't have more of them in our army.

In general, I took little part in these discussions. One day, I told my neighbours a story that I'd read in one of the books in the library, as it had particularly struck me. It concerned a certain Roshchepei,[9] who was a second-class soldier in the Russian Army at the start of the twentieth century. He worked as a blacksmith in a workshop where weapons were repaired, and it was here that he created one of his first models of automatic weapon, based on the principle of the fixed barrel and the movable breechblock. This was something new at the time. Unfortunately, the military hierarchy did not appreciate this invention as much as it should have done, and even viewed it as useless. As a result of this lack of understanding on the part of the Russian High Command, other countries benefited from Roshchepei's invention. The mechanism of the movable breechblock was copied in the Schwartzlose machine guns in Austria, and in the automatic rifle designed by the American Pedersen.

As for Federov, even before the First World War, he worked on a weapon halfway between a rifle and a machine gun, that he called an 'assault rifle'. But, just like Roshchepei, he didn't meet with the approval of the military authorities. In 1916, only a single small unit was equipped with Federov's automatic weapons. The first Soviet sub-machine gun was created at the end of the 1920s by Tokarev, who began his career in a locksmith's workshop.

As for Degtyarev, he started working at the age of 11 in a factory in Tula. Before the war, he received the medal of a Hero of Socialist Labour and the Hammer and Sickle medal. The latter of these bore the number 2. One day, as we were talking about this medal, one of the patients in the hospital shouted out, 'so who was number 1, then?' A heavy silence fell. Finally, it was broken by somebody saying, 'Are you a total idiot or are you winding us up? You mean you don't know who's number 1 in our country?'

'Comrade Stalin?'

'Bravo! Bit slow on the uptake, aren't you?'

I remembered this conversation much later, during Gorbachev's perestroika, when I was decorated with the medal for Best Industrial Entrepreneur, bearing the number 2. I asked everyone: 'So who's received medal number 1?' I'm still waiting for the answer . . .

*   *   *

While in hospital, I studied all known automatic weapons with the help of the parachutist lieutenant. We made careful drawings of them so as to understand better how they were made. I was trying to find my own path in the design of a new and revolutionary sub-machine gun. I longed for a chance to test out my ideas. But my wound was taking a very long time to heal, and my arm still wouldn't do what I wanted it to.

The doctors finally decided that there was no point in my staying in hospital, but that I was still far from being able to return to the front. Their conclusion was that I should take sick leave for several months. I was very disappointed – I'd have preferred to get back to the fighting at the front! But the doctors refused point blank. I needed a lot of rest if my right arm was ever going to get its strength back.

So I packed my bags, gathered my few meagre belongings, and in particular made sure I took with me my 'treasure': my drawings, my formulae, all the notes I'd taken on weapons. And I set off for the Altai, and my home village of Kurya.

'YOU MUST HELP SERGEANT KALASHNIKOV!'

In a compartment crammed with soldiers, I couldn't even stand up, as the pain in my shoulder was so intolerable. It was winter, and icy cold. A blind soldier was playing the harmonica, a sad song about an unfortunate Russian soldier who'd gone off to war without a rifle. And all of a sudden, I had a sort of flash of inspiration. It wasn't Kurya I should be going to, but Kazakhstan: the railway depot in the little town of Matai, where I had worked with my friend Gavril before the war. That was the only place where they could help me fulfil my plans.

A few days later, I found myself in the office of the depot chief. As it was wartime, the depot worked 24 hours a day, with the teams operating on a permanent rota. My military certificate gave me the right to have a certain number of food rations, which were more than enough for me to live on; and I had a document stipulating that they must 'help Sergeant Kalashnikov'.

By a fortunate coincidence, the depot manager was also named Kalashnikov: for me, this was a sign of destiny. Oddly, I felt quite at ease with him, almost a member of the family! I showed him the notebooks with the sketches of my future weapon. I managed to convince him, in spite of my bandaged arm that he glanced at with a doubtful expression. 'If you manage to find someone who's prepared to spare you a bit of his time, well, why not?' he said. Anyway, he gave me permission to use his workshop and his installations to carry out my project. Nobody in the depot thought I was really going to succeed, but, in wartime, it was difficult to refuse a wounded man who wanted to develop a new weapon.

I did actually need a little team of workers, with different specializations. I imagined I'd be able to do the engineering work all by myself. I didn't realize how complex the task of a weapons designer could be. I was very naive!

Finally, I managed to get together the workers I needed. An engineer would have viewed it as the work of a rather crazy amateur. But they believed in the project 100 per cent, and were even prepared to work at night.

The military chief of the region presented us with a Mosin rifle, so that I could make use of some of its pieces. Gradually, the whole thing took shape. For three months we worked really hard on this weapon, the first I ever designed!

* * *

I also had the good fortune to come across some extraordinary men. The depot manager gave me a room where I could live and work. A notice was put on my door, saying: 'No entry: special working group'. I had a pal, Genia Kravchenko, a specialist with a magic touch. With Genia we worked on my project. We would try out the prototype by firing it in the room itself. The place was less busy at night, which meant we could take pot shots as often as we wanted. In spite of everything, our working conditions were still precarious. If they'd been 'better', everything would have gone much more quickly. But we were convinced of the importance our sub-machine gun would have in the future. We were very proud of our first attempt, and even thought that it would bring us closer to victory over the fascist armies.

The head of the regional military commissariat examined my prototype and then took the decision to send 'sergeant Kalashnikov and his weapon' to Alma-Ata, a place I already knew as I'd stayed there before my military service. During the war, for fear of seeing Moscow fall into the hands of the Germans, the authorities had moved strategic organizations away to far-flung regions. Several factories, educational and research institutes had been transferred there, and many had come together in the hinterland, especially in Alma-Ata.

At the military commissariat of Alma-Ata, a young adjutant, sitting behind a big table, gave me a frosty reception. However, I greeted him very respectfully. 'Allow me to introduce myself: Sergeant-Major Kalashnikov, on sick leave. I've designed a new type of weapon, which I've brought with me. I'd be very grateful if you could inform the head of the military commissariat.'

He must have thought I was crazy, holding my submachine gun! Before I even had time to draw breath, I found myself in a cramped, musty little room. It was, of course, the gaol cell. The guards took my weapon off me, and even my belt. I spent much longer in this unpleasant place than in police detention in Kurya for carrying an illegal weapon. Four interminable days! I begged everyone who left that sinister spot to tell my friends where I was so they could get me out of there. At last, on the fourth day, the door opened, and the young adjutant who had locked me up appeared. In some embarrassment, he returned my personal effects to me as well as the sub-machine gun. He very politely informed me that a car was waiting for me downstairs. 'I've received orders to take you to the Central Committee of the Party in Kazakhstan. The secretary of the Central Committee in charge of military industry will receive you in person', the driver announced.

At first glance, I saw that the dignitary in question was trying to imitate Stalin. He was wearing a military-style costume and boots, and he seemed attentive to the least words and gestures of his interlocutor. He immediately realized that my sub-machine gun, manufactured in rather basic conditions, needed to be worked on, and that all the technical documentation still needed to be done. He gently explained that he wanted to introduce me to an engineer who was professor at the Moscow avionics faculty, whose students would be able to help me complete my sketches and calculations. The faculty had good workshops. I couldn't believe how lucky I was; a few hours earlier, I'd still been languishing in my prison cell. I was as happy as could be.

The dean of the faculty, Andrey Kazakov, immediately took me under his wing. A special team was set up to work on my sub-machine gun: it included a professor and a group of brilliant students from the higher classes. Our working space was 18 metres square, inside a little dilapidated house. As in the army, this was our living-quarters too, and we left the workshop only once a week, to go to the public baths.

The work progressed quickly. We rapidly made several quite significant improvements to the prototype. The model I'd created in the rail depot at Matai had a movable breech-block, which simplified the manufacture of the weapon, but at the same time led to several drawbacks. For example, the weight of the breechblock meant that the weapon was unbalanced. In Alma-Ata, we created a semi-movable breechblock, which enabled us to make it lighter. One day, an army general came to see our work. He was very impressed by the principle behind my sub-machine gun. He decided this project should definitely be given the go-ahead. It was decided I should go to Samarkand, in Uzbekistan, where the Dzherzhinksy Artillery Academy had provisionally been transferred. The celebrated professor Blagonravov would receive me.[10] I had never set foot in Uzbekistan before – another Soviet republic that would mark my life.

Anatoli Arkadyevich Blagonravov was a great specialist in automatic firearms. I'd read some of his works while I was trying to deepen my theoretical understanding during my stay in hospital. I knew entire pages of his works off by heart. He was stupefied to learn that I hadn't had any specialist education, and even more by the fact that my sub-machine gun had been built in simple workshops in a railway depot, and completed in another poorly equipped place. He asked me various questions, both about my work and about my private life. I was flattered that he should take such an interest in my personality. I felt that this great scientist was really taking my destiny to his heart. He was a highly cultivated man, one of the 'old school'. In my presence, he wrote two letters. The gist of these was that my sub-machine gun, as it was, couldn't be recommended for mass production because the design was too complex and didn't altogether correspond to the prevailing technical norms; but its originality showed that Sergeant Kalashnikov was a talented autodidact, who should be given the possibility of pursuing specialized studies, since one day he could certainly become a good designer. He even suggested giving me a bonus! This was on 2 July 1942.

Finally, the military authorities decided that this wasn't the moment for me to pursue my studies, and that right now it was more important to improve and complete my weapon. I was sent to Moscow, to the Main Artillery Directorate.

The head of the Inventions Department told me: 'There's no better place to continue work on your prototype than the Shurovo Polygon, in the Moscow region. I'm going to give orders for them to help you complete your project. There you'll be able to carry out studies and carry out all the trials you need to.'

In the train that took me there, my travelling companion was none other than the great weapons designer Simonov, whose name was known to all those in the military, even before the war.[11] The hierarchy had asked him to 'take me under his wing', which he was only too glad to do. He had designed the AVS automatic rifle. Legend has it that, at the start of the war, when the German tanks were sowing panic, Simonov had been personally instructed by Stalin to create the first design for an anti-tank rifle – which he had done in 22 sleepless days and nights.

We met up again a few years later, towards the end of the war, this time as competitors. We both found ourselves in front of a jury to which we were presenting models of automatic-loading rifles. Simonov won this competition, beating several competitors, including myself.

The rifle on which Simonov was working became famous throughout the world. It was unequalled in any country. This was the weapon that everyone could see, on television or in magazine photos, in the hands of the Kremlin guards at 'Post No. 1', Lenin's mausoleum.

The Shurovo Polygon impressed me with its magnificent museum, and its very extensive collection of weapons, unique in the whole USSR. There were Russian and foreign models from previous centuries, as well as the latest models of Soviet weapons, of course. Thanks to the prototypes on display, I was able to study the evolution of firearms and their construction techniques. This gave me plenty to think about. The museum also included weapons which had not been chosen for mass production. Despite this, they were of great interest: some of them were highly original, and made me ponder what it was they were lacking for them to be used in the army. This was the main source of my studies after military hospital.

It was the destiny of my very first sub-machine gun to end up in a museum too. It is currently on display in the Museum of Military History in Saint Petersburg. This prototype is very dear to me – it's like a child I brought into the world amid the suffering and privations of wartime.

Despite the fact that none of my weapons won any of those various competitions, my chiefs still had every confidence in me and suggested that I get to work on a light machine gun, which several designers were already involved with. I had already created the prototype of a light machine gun at the Matai depot. But the competition was fierce. They decided to send me to Tashkent, the capital of Uzbekistan, to manufacture my model. I was allocated a team of specialized workers, as well as a workshop and all the necessary equipment.

The deadline for the prototype to be submitted was 15 December 1943: I would be just 24 at that date. I was still a staff sergeant, but I already enjoyed the status of a professional arms designer. As a result, I picked up a salary of 1,500 roubles per month.

So here I was back at the Polygon. This time, the jury had to decide between three designs of light machine gun: Simonov's, Degtyarev's and mine. Unfortunately, yet again, my design was not selected. Thus it was that my light machine gun ended up in the museum, just like my first sub-machine gun!

My pride was terribly hurt, even though Degtyarev was also eliminated straightaway – and although Simonov's model was initially selected, it eventually failed in the trials. I kept mulling over the reasons for these two failures. And I realized several things: ease of handling is essential in the development of a weapon, as is the simplicity of its different components and its overall reliability. I also realized that it was important not to use small components, as they could be lost during dismantling.

Still, my faith in my talent as a designer had been shaken by my poor results. Not only that: some of my mates started to take the mickey out of me. 'Are you sure weapons design is really your thing?' I wanted to return to the front, but my boss categorically refused, and told me off. 'What you're doing isn't easy. I suppose you think it would be easier just to give up right now? But just think it over: if you stay here, you could maybe invent a weapon that could be used by entire divisions. A weapon that could make a decisive contribution to our victory. We intend to send you to Central Asia to carry on with your work.'

3

THE BIRTH OF THE AK

After the victory of Stalingrad, at the start of 1943, the Soviet Army launched an offensive on all fronts. The siege of Leningrad, the heroic city that had resisted every enemy attack, was lifted. The Crimea and most of the Ukraine were liberated. In 1944, the Red Army drove the invaders from Soviet territory and, under the command of Marshal Zhukov, entered Warsaw and took the banks of the Oder. In May 1945, Prague and Vienna were liberated, and the unconditional surrender of Nazi Germany was signed by Zhukov and Keitel. Japan in turn surrendered on August 1945, but did not officially surrender with a signed document until 2 September.

The spectacular victory parade on Red Square, and the triumphant military procession, filled the Soviets and their allies with euphoria.

However, the losses and the damage inflicted by the Germans during the four years of war were enormous. Soviet historians put their deaths at 5 million; Western historians suggest that the figure is closer to 20 million. In addition to the damage *caused by the war, a terrible drought struck the country in 1946. A million people died of hunger and other privations; despite this, Stalin continued to fly in the face of common sense by exporting wheat. The situation improved in 1947 – so dramatically that food ration cards were abolished.*

The next problem was converting military industry back to civilian use. The USSR returned to its pre-1940 economic model. To emerge from the crisis, Soviet power demanded ever greater efforts on the part of the population. The Gulag was forced to increase its production capacity several times over. From 1946 onwards, the 'nomenklatura' was all-powerful: the number of senior bureaucrats increased to seven times what it had been in 1928. Three years after victory, production caught up with its pre-war levels.

Ever since the Revolution, priests had been persecuted and churches destroyed, barbarically and systematically. Stalin even blew up the majestic Cathedral of Christ the Saviour, right in the middle of Moscow (it was reconstructed much later, during the 1990s, thanks to the efforts of the Mayor of Moscow, Yuri Luzhkov).

When war broke out, Stalin had a brilliantly inspired idea: he summoned the church to his aid, so that it could stimulate the patriotism of its faithful flock. Stalin's aim was to draw a line under the past; now the whole Soviet population was to join in the struggle against the invader. As in the time of the Tsars, the army went off into battle with the blessing of the Patriarch.

Shortly after the victory, Stalin gradually returned to his pre-war anti-clerical policies. The power of security organizations increased perceptibly. The Central Committee of the Party took over the control of the intelligentsia. Stalin's favourite academician, Lysenko, denounced genetic research as 'anti-scientific'.

During the war, Stalin's repressions were much less in evidence. But from 1946 onwards, they resumed on an even greater scale. The struggle against 'cosmopolitans' provoked a wave of anti-Semitism. It was directly linked to the birth of the State of Israel, considered to be pro-American. The President of the Jewish Antifascist Committee, Michoels, was assassinated, and this served as the pretext for a new trial whose victims were not just the members of this committee, but also other artists and writers.

The cult of Stalin now assumed gigantic proportions.

THE 'MIKHTIM' DOSSIER

So here I was, off on my travels again: Alma-Ata, then Tashkent. All these places – Matai, Alma-Ata, Tashkent, Samarkand, Moscow and the Shurovo Polygon, had become familiar and much-loved places to me, since they had marked the essential stages in my life.

The more I worked, the more experience I built up. I was finding my path. When I returned to the Polygon, I settled down to a new project: making an automatic rifle. It was a meeting with Simonov, who was working on just such a model, that led my thoughts in that direction.

Subsequently, I obtained a mission order, signed by Marshal Voronov, which assigned me to the Inventions Department. This mission confirmed my status as a designer. I never forgot that I had got no further than seventh year at school; but it isn't always paper qualifications that determine how much you know. My research on this rifle gave me an occasion to bounce back. I think that if Simonov's rifle hadn't existed, mine might perhaps have been accepted.

I'd drawn inspiration from the American Garand rifle, which loaded automatically.[1] The originality of my plan consisted in including this rifle's mechanism for automatically discarding empty cartridges, but with a few modifications.

The result wasn't bad. However, yet again, my attempts were to meet with failure.

I had the bad luck, during the trials, to get on the wrong side of a very impulsive major-general, who wanted to try out my prototype himself. Some targets were set up, and the weapon was loaded to maximum capacity. After a few bursts of gunfire, the ammunition had all been used up, and the magazine was thrown aside. Instead of loading a new magazine, the general started looking for something in the grass: he seemed irritated. We realized he was looking for the empty magazine. But the originality of my weapon resided precisely in the fact that the old magazine was automatically discarded. When I told him he shouldn't be looking for the empty magazine but picking up a new one, he flew into a rage. 'Of course! *I* understand that – but will an ordinary soldier understand? He's going to think it's a piece of the rifle that's fallen off. You're a young designer, Kalashnikov, and if you're only interested in being original at any price, then don't bother coming back here.' I thought his words were very unfair, but I learnt from this lesson, and I drew certain conclusions that were useful later on for my assault rifle, the AK.

It was also during this period that I got to know an exceptional designer, Aleksei Sudayev.[2] Although he'd already been decorated with the Order of Lenin and that of the Red Star, he was hardly more than 30 years old. Without knowing it, I was 'squatting' in his office. One fine day, he came up behind me and shouted, 'Oh, is that how it is, people working in my office without my permission!' I was embarrassed, but he didn't bear me any grudges.

Sudayev's sub-machine gun, put into service in 1942, was the best of the Second World War. No foreign weapon could match it in simplicity, reliability and effectiveness in combat. Sudayev had designed it in Leningrad, while the city was being besieged by Hitler's armies. It is hard to believe that the weapon was actually built in Leningrad during a total blockade.

So my design for a rifle never got any further than the trial stage, but I used its most interesting characteristics in my new project. Several designers were already working on an assault rifle. The pioneer in this domain was again Aleksei Sudayev: he'd already started to create weapons that used this type of ammunition at the start of 1944.

Sudayev had a highly developed analytical sense, and he had realized before everyone else that automatic weapons required an altogether new approach. Designers needed to alter their whole mindset, since the sub-machine guns of the period didn't live up to the demands for effectiveness made on them in terms of distance and aim. The first series of Sudayev assault rifles that rolled out of the Soviet factories in 1945 had one drawback: their weight. Some means of making them lighter had to be found. So Sudayev continued to work unremittingly on his project.

*   *   *

A competition was launched in 1945 to devise a new assault rifle, equipped with a completely new type of ammunition, smaller than that used in a rifle, but bigger than in a pistol.

The competition was anonymous: each of the participants worked under a pseudonym. The aim was to obtain an objective decision from the jury, uninfluenced by the prestige attaching to a famous name. I found it very difficult to make up my mind to take part in this competition. After all, it was rather a bold thing for me to do – how could I, without any specialized studies behind me, stand any chance of winning such a challenge, when all the great Soviet designers of the period were taking part?

I made a hundred or so sketches of different components. I was helped by several specialists, a team comprising several industrial technicians and draughtsmen. We were all very young. We were intent on showing that our youth could be an additional asset; we were brimful of energy, and sometimes worked until midnight.

My previous model for an automatic rifle was of great help to us. The most original component we wanted to include in our plan for this new weapon in fact came from that previous rifle, with a few slight modifications: the whole locking apparatus of the bore of the piece of ordnance. After weeks of unremitting labour, the outlines of my future weapon started to appear. It attracted the attention of the officers in the Polygon. They gave me advice and criticism, and helped me with some of the technical calculations.

Destiny was watching over me, and provided me with some valuable help. I'd made the acquaintance of a young draughtswoman with whom I fell in love. Her name was Katya Moiseyeva. She applied herself wholeheartedly to drawing, with the most extreme precision, the sketches that I entrusted her with, and this enabled me to present a very carefully thought-out plan to the jury.

In the end, the AK was the first fruit of our love.

Once the technical drawings had been finished and the calculations completed, I had to find a pseudonym to sign my work with. One of my friends suggested putting the first syllable of my forename with that of my patronymic, Mikhail Timofeyevich, to produce 'Mikhtim'. I was a bit perplexed at the idea; as a young sergeant, I wasn't used to people addressing me by my patronymic, a formula traditionally reserved for NCOs and senior officers. Still, this was the pseudonym I chose. The entire dossier on my proposed weapon, with drawings and calculations, and signed 'Mikhtim', was sent to the jury in Moscow.

The wait for the reply seemed to go on forever. One fine day, the door opened and I heard a woman's voice that had become very dear to me. It was Katya. With a put-on air of severity, she shook my hand. 'Our department has asked me to convey our congratulations to you: your project has been selected by the jury.' I didn't believe a word of it! I was used to my friends making fun of me, but I thought that this time they really were going a bit too far. I turned my back on her by way of protest; Katya was irritated, and stormed off. In her place, a group of my mates, fizzing with excitement, came bursting into my office. 'Well Mikhtim, aren't you going to offer us a glass of something to toast your success? Don't worry, we're not going to let you off!'

In the staff headquarters, I received official confirmation that the project signed by Mikhtim had been selected for the rest of the competition. Now I had to make this weapon in metal, and proceed to the next stage with the other winners of the contest. All the personnel in the Polygon got to hear of my growing success. Wherever I went, I heard them whispering, 'Mikhtim, Mikhtim . . .'

In 1946, at the next stage of the competition, Sudayev, who of course was still the favourite to win, died suddenly. His model had already passed trials in the army, and a small series of them had actually been built. In my view, if Aleksei Sudayev had lived longer, he would have managed to obtain some exceptional results. In a few years, this peerless designer had achieved more than most of his colleagues did in their whole lives.

There were only three competitors left in the running: Baryshev, Rukavishnikov and myself. The most experienced of the three was, quite incontestably, the engineer-colonel Nikolai Vassilyevich Rukavishnikov. He was already well known before the war, in particular for the way he had developed anti-tank weapons. Lieutenant Baryshev, also an engineer, was even younger than I was: he was only 23. We were all competing, but we sometimes swapped advice.

I enjoyed my work as a designer at the Polygon enormously. The task of designing new weapons galvanized me; I felt in incredible shape, and I was passionate about my research. In my view, if the talent of a designer is going to be widely acknowledged, he needs the right conditions to be met. The most important is that he should freely choose the objective of his work. He must be able to benefit from the experience of his predecessors and have the necessary material means at his disposal. This may appear obvious, but it hasn't always been the case. Our Polygon fulfilled these conditions. Within its perimeter, where healthy competition flourished, everything was so designed as to enable each designer to give of his best.

Once my product had been given the go-ahead, I was supposed to be provided with a workshop to build my model in metal. Unfortunately, I had to leave the Polygon provisionally, simply because the workshops were already occupied. I went to the Kovrov factory, north-east of Moscow – a town that specialized in weapons construction, like Tula and Izhevsk.[3] It was here that the Degtyarev team was working at the time. The famous weapons designer Degtyarev, who was to be my rival, was then a general, 66 years old. This caused me some anxiety. Paradoxically, during the whole year I was working there, I never even met him. We each worked on our respective models as if someone had erected a wall between us.

These days, a factory in Kovrov bears the name of Degtyarev. Back then, there were already legends circulating about him. Stalin had personally presented him with a superb car, one of the prestigious ZIS models. The story went that, so as to impress an important audience at a particular meeting, he'd arrived on the podium in his car, and this had involved knocking down the wall at the back of the building. Then he'd emerged from his enormous black ZIS, in the full uniform of a general, covered with all his medals.

A year later, for the next stage in the competition, I returned to my dear Polygon in the environs of Moscow, where I was overjoyed to be reunited with my Katya. Several designers from all over the country were arriving. I saw Degtyarev climbing out of his car, not sparing a glance for those around him, completely absorbed by his thoughts. Shpagin was there too (I recognized him from the photos I'd seen in the press.) Together with Simonov, we all met up like old acquaintances, as we did with Rukavishnikov and Baryshev, who had stayed on in the Polygon all this time. Once again, I felt completely intimidated. I kept telling myself, 'Just take a look at your opponents. You may as well pack your bags: no point in wasting your time!' I didn't really think I had much chance of winning.

What the jury was mainly looking for was a weapon that would shoot accurately, be reliable and have the right calibre and weight, resistant components and a simple structure. Our 'client', the Main Artillery Directorate, was our supreme judge.

The designers all behaved in very different ways while the members of the jury were carrying out the trials on their weapons. Degtyarev assumed an air of detachment, and paraded his indifference towards the trials. He seemed to be constantly prey to new ideas. Shpagin, on the other hand, kept minutely analysing the measurements of his weapon's firing speed. Bulkin kept a close eye on the slightest moves his rivals made, and was forever checking that his prototype was clean. He looked as if he was afraid someone might put a spoke in his wheels. Other designers concealed their stress by chatting to each other. I fell into this group, but I didn't feel in the slightest bit like laughing and joking, even if I was usually the life and soul of the party. Niels Bohr was right when he wrote that there are things that are so serious you can only joke about them.

The final results of all the trials were closely studied by the appropriate commission. Their conclusions were severe. Shpagin realized that his model had no chance of winning, and withdrew. Degtyarev's model didn't produce good results either.

Several models were eliminated out of hand, and the commission didn't even recommend them as worth developing. Three others, including mine, were lucky enough to take part in the subsequent trials. We had to work on improving our models, in accordance with the jury's recommendations, but we were still in the running. Obviously, we knew that, out of the three of us, only one would get across the final hurdle.

It was at this time that I finally won Katya's heart for good. A year of separation had proved that we couldn't live without each other. Unfortunately, it was impossible for her to come with me, and I had to leave alone, even if we were unofficially married. Still, I felt doubly happy and proud: I was in love, and I was making a victorious return to Kovrov to carry on with my work.

Here I was given a triumphant reception by my team. Many of them started to believe I might win, and Commander Deykin managed to persuade the best specialists in the factory to help me in my task.

'UP UNTIL 2025, AND EVEN BEYOND . . .'

It was during this period that I came up with several new ideas that turned my life upside-down. I completely altered the general structure of my weapon. As the rules of the competition didn't allow me to change its overall design, I had to pretend that I was working on a mere improvement. Sasha Zaitsev, my faithful right-hand man from the start of the competition, was at this time the only person aware of my real plan. The changes I was envisaging weren't provided for in the conditions laid down for the competition, but they did simplify the structure of the weapon and increased its reliability when used in difficult conditions: dampness, sand, jungle . . . We did actually end up telling General Deykin – he entirely approved of my reasons. He was a great specialist in firearms; his advice was invaluable. He played his role in what was to become the AK-47.

Zaytsev and I could hardly sleep. We dedicated all our time to making new components. We created a breechblock shutter in a single piece, with a shaft. We redesigned the trigger mechanism, as well as the cover of the breechblock unit, so that it now completely enclosed the movable pieces. We succeeded in solving the problem of the safety catch. It now had several functions: it ensured the change from automatic position to the shot-by-shot position and the safety catch. In addition, it protected the breechblock unit from dust and other kinds of dirt.

The factory mechanics immediately realized that the new pieces were much simpler and more reliable than the old ones. Finally, our design represented a real leap forward in the history of automatic weapons construction. We broke all the stereotypes that had dominated the field.

There has always been something idiosyncratic about the creative process of the weapons designer. His art consists of assembling, within a limited set of parameters and with a given mass, a series of components that will enable him to obtain the desired result in terms of reliability, ease of handling, shelf life and precision. The components themselves have existed for a long time, being developed and modernized from century to century. Some of them, still usable today, were invented in the seventeenth century, and even earlier. It's very difficult – even for an experienced engineer – to develop them these days, or to create new

ones. The essential thing is to build up a coherent whole, to
share the component parts out in the optimum way so as to
make them interact effectively. This process of creation
demands from the designer a highly developed visualization
of three-dimensional space.

Weapons all look alike, as do people. Everyone has eyes,
arms, legs, etc. And yet every person is unique. My assault
rifle is based on completely different principles from, for
instance, its German counterpart. All my prototypes are different from one another, but the basis remains the same. For
example, the locking apparatus of the weapon's bore is
always the same, and the rest varies with each different
model. This locking apparatus is quite similar to Garand's
model, without being altogether identical to it.

Our great designer Tokarev had adopted one principle
which determined the overall shape of his weapons: all the
elements were stuck to one another so that not even dust
could get in. My approach is different: all the elements are
spaced out, as if they were hanging in air. In this way, even if
the weapon falls into sand, the mechanism isn't affected.

Our new model, for all its advantages, didn't conform to
the jury's demands either, especially as regards the length of
the barrel: this had gone from 500 mm to 420 mm. On the
other hand, the total length of the weapon was in accordance
with their demands.

Thus we were running the risk of quite simply being eliminated from the competition, but we thought that the commission wouldn't notice this 'deception' straightaway. We
knew perfectly well that someone would eventually spot it,
but we hoped that this would only happen as late as possible,
when the weapon had already proved its superiority.

One of the first to have seen this 'revolutionary' model
was my rival, General Degtyarev himself. Before the final
stage of the trials, the representatives of our client went to

the Kovrov factory, and they made a point of introducing me to Degtyarev. It was the first time I'd ever spoken to him. 'Come on then, cards on the table!' someone joked. 'I suggest each of you shows his model to the other.'

We were in complete agreement and only too happy to present our weapons to one another – those weapons we'd been slaving away over for so many days and nights. Degtyarev looked very tired to me, but his face lit up when he saw my prototype. He examined each component of my weapon (which I had dismantled specially for the occasion) with the greatest attention. The breechblock shutter in particular met with his approval, as well as the cover of the breechblock unit. He also thought that my safety catch was very original in design.

Meanwhile, I in turn was examining his assault rifle, which seemed a bit heavy to me. And all of a sudden, General Degtyarev made this staggering declaration: 'The way Sergeant Kalashnikov has put the components of his model together is much more ingenious than in mine. His model has more of a future – of that I'm certain. I no longer wish to participate in the final phase of the competition.'

He'd said all that loud enough for everyone to hear. I can remember the moment perfectly well. The general was in uniform, decorated with his medal, the star of a Hero of Socialist Labour. I think that it was very brave of him to think in this way. It was an act of great honesty, and indeed nobility – especially in view of the fact that he was one of the 'favourites' of the regime. He could have taken advantage of his situation, as did so many others, who used their fame to throw their weight around in competitions.

Our client's representatives did eventually persuade Degtyarev to take part in the last phase of the competition, but he left early on, once the first trials were over. That left just three competitors in the running: Bulkin, Dementyev and myself.

The commission only discovered the irregularities in my assault rifle once the trials were resumed, just as they were evaluating its aim. Suddenly, an engineer grabbed a ruler, measured the length of the barrel and started quite simply to roar, 'But the barrel is 80 mm shorter than it's supposed to be! You've contravened the competition rules! You're going to be disqualified!'

However, since nobody could deny that our results were the best when it came to precision of aim, the commission finally took the decision to allow us to stay in the competition.

All the same, I was given a warning: I was told to ensure I didn't depart from the straight and narrow again – I had to observe the jury's requirements. This didn't spoil my satisfaction, since my weapon had demonstrated its reliability from the start. There was never any interruption in the firing, and the crowning glory was that I found it more elegant than the others.

The trials were becoming harder and harder: we had to stick the loaded assault rifles into swamps, or drag them through sand before firing them. The sand got into the mechanisms. Our weapon was the one that put up best with this rough treatment. This was, I believe, to a large degree thanks to the way we had reorganized the components with Zaytsev.

The advantages of my modifications were blindingly obvious. I was jubilant. The new cover of the breechblock unit and the new security catch not only fulfilled their main roles well, but also meant that the weapon was even more reliable. They protected it from sand, mud and water.

The testing of the weapon's reliability and resistance continued. The latest trial involved it being thrown, in different positions, onto a cement floor. After impact, the weapon was checked out to see if everything had remained intact in the mechanism.

Once all the firing trials had been completed, the results were scrupulously verified by the appropriate commission. At this point I'd like to quote the weapons expert Malimon:

In accordance with the new tactical and technical norms of the Main Directorate of Artillery (1945), the following designers devised, built and presented for testing at the Polygon competition their designs for an assault rifle: N. V. Rukavishnikov, M. T. Kalashnikov, A. A. Bulkin, A. A. Dementyev and G. A. Korobov. The trials were carried out between 30 June and 12 August 1947, by a commission chaired by N. S. Okhnotnikov, in accordance with the instructions issued by I. I. Litichevsky.

Simultaneously, comparative trials were carried out on the machine gun AS-44 designed by Sudayev, the PPSh-41 designed by Shpagin, and the German MP-44.

V. A. Degtyarev was anxious not to be left behind: he submitted for testing a light machine gun that could be used as a portable weapon or on a tripod. This light machine gun was based on the principle, already in vogue among designers, of swivel locking, and loading by strips of cartridges. But, for various reasons, this system was in the end not put into mass production.

As a result of the first trial results, the commission selected the models of Kalashnikov, Dementyev and Bulkin. For the next stage of the competition, the designers were recommended to increase the precision of aim and the rapidity of firing, to decrease the weight and the bore of the weapons, and to increase their resistance.

The commission of the jury reached the following conclusions:

1 None of the assault rifles presented is in accordance with the TTT norms of the Main Artillery Directorate, and none of them can be recommended for mass production.

2 The assault rifles of Kalashnikov (with pressed breechblock unit), Dementyev and Bulkin attained the closest results to the TTT norms, and have been selected for further development. This is to be carried out with complete respect for the conclusions of the present report.

This conclusion was confirmed by a decision of the General Staff of Soviet Armed Forces as dated 10 October 1947.

If 1947 was a decisive year for me, it was also a turning-point in the life of our country. In the context of the Cold War, it was a turning-point in the defence capabilities of the USSR: it was in this year that Soviet scientists discovered the formula for the atomic bomb. It was also the year of monetary reform, and the year in which ration cards were abolished.

On 10 January 1948, a meeting of the technical and scientific commission of the Polygon was held. None of the 13 members contested the fact that the Kalashnikov assault rifle best fulfilled all their demands.

And I'm proud of the fact – why should I conceal it? Over 50 years of use, weapons based on the AK-47 model have incontestably proved its mettle in combat. In all the assault weapons and light machine guns designed during the second half of the twentieth century, both in Russia and in other countries, you will find components copied from the AK. And even these days, it is evident that Kalashnikovs produced in the 1950s are in perfect working condition.

*   *   *

Certain people would like to cast doubt on the paternity of the AK-47. The scandal rag *Moskovskiy Komsomolets* recently published a would-be sensational article. The AK-47, which I finalized in the Kovrov factory, was quite unlike its predecessor, the AK-46: so said these defamatory remarks. They insinuated that I'd taken advantage of the work of Bulkin and Dementyev, my competitors. The authors slyly suggested that I had 'pinched' elements of their weapons. I'm 83 years old, but unfortunately I'm still here to reply to those mendacious accusations! This is what I did in an article in the same paper.

Each competitor had his own original plans for a new weapon. This information was crucial and confidential, and nobody apart from the designer himself could divulge it.

I appreciated my colleagues' work at its true value. They too were working on automatic weapons, using ammunition whose prototype version went back to 1943. Before working on the AK, I'd designed a light machine gun and an automatic-loading rifle, in which there were already pieces and mechanisms that I later used in the AK. I always had an opinion of my own on important questions, but I listened attentively to the advice of my colleagues and of military specialists. I meticulously analysed all the components and mechanisms of Russian and foreign weapons available in our Polygon. Each of the participants in the competition had the possibility of studying all these weapons and comparing them with the one he was building. Like the others, I drew inspiration from what I saw. I won't deny, for instance, that I borrowed an idea from Garand.

In order to obtain the most effective interplay of components and mechanisms, I had to work and rework my prototype several times over before presenting it in the official competition. Each one of us put in some very hard work, but only a few were lucky enough to make it through to the final. Naturally, I am grateful to my colleagues and the military specialists who helped me, since it is obvious that I didn't have enough technical know-how to bring this project to a successful conclusion all by myself. I agree with what has been written about me by the American arms expert and historian Edward C. Ezell[4] in his book *The AK-47 Story*: 'He had a born gift as a designer. But he depended on his colleagues' knowledge. These were the people who enabled him to complete his project, his first and most important invention, the AK-47.'

Up until now I have been awarded more than 50 certificates acknowledging my priority as the inventor both of different weapons components and of entire weapons. I received five of these certificates even before I started work on the AK: so I had the basis I needed. Several components of my previous inventions, having been reworked and improved, were used in the AK. But whenever I got a better idea, I would abandon the old version without regret.

Like other designers, I met with failure and success. It's just that, after the creation of the AK-47, I had many more successes than failures.

* * *

The very next day after the announcement of the Commission's decision, I left for Izhevsk, together with Sasha Zaytsev and Lieutenant-Colonel Deykin. The only thing on our minds was the production of a first series of AK-47s. It still had to undergo trials in the army. It often happened that the career of certain weapons came to a halt at this stage.

This first series was thus to be built in a factory in Izhevsk, 1,000 kilometres or so east of Moscow – in other words, some 20 hours by train. Originally, it wasn't a weapons factory, but a place where they manufactured motorbikes! I didn't know at the time that I would be spending the rest of my life in this city of Izhevsk.

The principal designer in the factory was called David Abramovich Vinokgoiz. He designated a group of engineers and specialized workers to work on my weapon. I took advantage of this occasion to tell him about my other plans. As well as my assault rifle, I was very keen to build some of my other models of automatic weapons, which I'd modernized. I managed to convince him quite quickly, and some of my other models were produced in the factory; unfortunately they never got past the trial stage. Still, this all helped us to optimize the performance of my AK-47.

I immediately struck up a friendship with Vinokgoiz. This friendship lasted 30 years, until his death.

The role of principal designer was fundamental: the factory produced in general up to ten different weapons models, and he was the person who had to deal with any problems in their manufacture.

The first series of my assault rifle was completed by the deadline and sent to Moscow. The quality of weapons coming out of the factory was impeccable. Two months later, I was summoned to the Main Artillery Directorate in Moscow. The artillery chief, Marshal Voronov himself, wanted to test out my weapon. Once I arrived in Moscow, I travelled by train with Voronov to the place where the trials were to be carried out. Voronov had his own personal wagon. In mine, there was a surprise for me: Degtyarev and Simonov were waiting. My assault rifle was going to be tested at the same time as Degtyarev's light machine gun and Simonov's automatic-loading rifle.

Voronov invited me to dine in his wagon. I was struck by the fact that he invited me alone, without Degtyarev or Simonov. I'd already met Voronov: ever since 1944, he had been the one who regularly gave his agreement to the financing of my different plans.

During dinner, I told him how I'd modified my weapon. I thanked him warmly for the indispensable financial aid he had provided me with. Voronov was a really nice guy!

Once we reached our destination, each of us settled into a room that we had been assigned for work and rest. Marshal Voronov made a point of presenting us to the soldiers. When my turn came, he took hold of me and from his great height he swept me up into the air!

'Allow me to introduce you to Sergeant Kalashnikov. He ought rather to be called Designer Kalashnikov. He's come to find out what you think about his assault rifle and any feedback you can give him.'

I was embarrassed, and blushing as red as beetroot, but the soldiers applauded me warmly. I think they were pleased that an ordinary soldier could be recognized as one of the great weapons designers.

I listened attentively to everything they had to tell me about my weapon. It appeared that it was too noisy: some people complained it gave them ear-ache which sometimes lasted three days after an intensive session of firing. I was only half surprised, since I was already aware of this defect. I knew how to tackle this problem, but I didn't do so, since I didn't dare infringe too far on the rules that governed its production. My solution was simply to remove the muzzle brake. Marshal Voronov thought this was an interesting possibility, and we tried it out there and then. The noise diminished perceptibly, and the weapon became more comfortable to fire. So it was put into mass production minus its muzzle brake.

Other soldiers were displeased at the fact that it was difficult to clean and oil certain components, in particular those of the trigger mechanism, which couldn't be dismantled.

I thought over these remarks a great deal, sharing my reflections with Degtyarev and Simonov, who told me about their own anxieties. They were then at the pinnacle of their fame. All three of us agreed that a designer's work is never done. Whatever you're doing, whether you're out for a walk or trying to relax, the need to improve your weapons never leaves you.

Degtyarev had just organized, in his factory at Kovrov, an exhibition displaying the weapons captured from the enemy. He explained the differences between Soviet and German weapons, and drew comparisons between them. He thought there were interesting things to be learnt from German weapons. There's nothing wrong with that. But this exhibition certainly demonstrated the superiority of Soviet firearms over those of Nazi Germany. It's worth remembering, for instance, that Degtyarev designed a light machine gun that equipped the Red Army from 1927 onwards, and it remained the standard for automatic weapons for two decades.

What brought us together, apart from our purely technical research, was our thirst for knowledge in every domain. All the Soviet weapons designers I've ever known have one point in common: they are people who like to educate themselves. Reading is one of their favourite pastimes. In addition to that, they almost all enjoy hunting and fishing, and nature in general. Weapons designers are men of passion – like myself. Perhaps that's what gives them such long lives. . .

*   *   *

The day before our departure, Voronov, who still lived in his wagon on a marshalling yard, once again summoned me to see him. There were ten or so officers with him. 'We'd like to hear your story, get to know something about your life, your origins, your family. We already know Degtyarev and Simonov pretty well. But we don't know you at all.'

This was my first 'press conference'. I obviously couldn't relate my real life story to them. If I had done so, I would surely not have been allowed to carry on with my career as a designer. God knows what might have happened to me. I wasn't going to tell them about my childhood as a deportee, the son of a kulak, an 'enemy of the people'. I came out with a story I'd prepared a long time in advance: in it, I 'omitted' certain details.

After this short meeting, Voronov told me I would spend the night in his wagon, and return with him to Moscow. The following morning, he asked me an important question: he wanted to know whether I wished to remain in the army or go over into civilian life, while continuing my career as a designer. Tokarev and Simonov were civilians, though this didn't stop them being well respected in army circles. Voronov apparently thought I was going to stay in the army and follow in Degtyarev's footsteps. But the fact was that I'd wanted to get out of army uniform for quite some time now. Katya had at last been able to join me, I already had two children, and I was eager to lead a less restricted life. The Marshal was evidently somewhat disappointed at my decision; still, he agreed to my request. And all at once, he asked me to leave my photo with him, autographed. Did he think my name would one day be famous?

*   *   *

Shortly afterwards, I set out again for Izhevsk, where my family and my factory were waiting for me. Uppermost in my mind was setting up and training a good team, with all sorts of specialists in it. The new objective was clear: mass production of my assault rifle, whose official name was '7.62 mm Kalashnikov assault rifle AK-47', the famous weapon that history remembers simply as the 'AK-47'. 'AK' are the initials of 'Avtomat Kalashnikova', which in Russian means 'Kalashnikov automatic assault rifle'; '47' of course designates the year I designed the model that was adopted by the army.

So the first series had been launched at the motorbike factory in Izhevsk. Subsequently, everything was transferred to another factory in Izhevsk, 'Izhmash',[5] which had been producing arms since the start of the previous century: indeed, it was with weapons made there that the Russians had fought against Napoleon's army during the Battle of Borodino in 1812.

That year, 1948, I was the first to come to the factory each morning, and the last to leave at night. The team was taking shape, slowly but surely. It often happened that we worked past midnight.

Although the assault rifle had been officially adopted and integrated into the equipment of the Soviet army, I was forever coming up with new ideas, which I wanted to put into practice. For instance, I intended to touch up one of the components, the breechblock, with which I wasn't altogether satisfied. This entailed the modification of several small pieces. But there was an obstacle: my superiors were often unwilling to accept the alterations I was proposing, since they were responsible for production and didn't want to take any risks. The army representative at the factory, despite being a friend of mine, completely refused to introduce this change into the assembly belt. So I was forced to resort to subterfuge: I patiently waited until he was on annual leave to include the new piece in the production process. When he returned, he faced a fait accompli – manufacture had already started! Still, he didn't hold it against me and resigned himself with good grace to the inevitable.

* * *

Nearly half a century later, for my 75th birthday, President Boris Yeltsin came to Izhevsk in person to offer his congratulations. He made a solemn speech, in which he talked, among other things, of making up for an injustice: my AK-47 wasn't patented, and he promised he'd remedy that situation, so that I would finally be able to receive the royalties from my assault rifle. But alas, he never did so!

Recently, several decades after the appearance of the first Kalashnikov, a weapon used throughout the entire world, our factory managed to obtain a patent. But it owes nothing to Yeltsin. Personally, I've never earned a kopek from arms sales. If the state had given me just one rouble for every Kalashnikov produced throughout the world, I'd have been able to help many young inventors.

These days, our factory in Izhevsk produces only a small number of Kalashnikovs; we tend to make hunting rifles, based on the Kalashnikov model. And the other countries that produce my weapon claim they are authorized to do so, since the USSR has purely and simply given it away. As a result I have never been – and I must insist on this – either involved in or interested in arms production or sales, whether in Russia or anywhere else!

*   *   *

Thus it is that, in just over two years, a new type of automatic weapon was put into production. Usually, a job like that took four to five years. Ezell, the American firearms historian, wrote: 'The appearance of Kalashnikov assault rifles on the world scene is one of the symbols of the new technological era that began in the USSR.' In his own words, 'a great invention in the domain of firearms first saw the day in the USSR. We can surmise that the Kalashnikov will probably be used until 2025, and even beyond.'

A UNIQUE WEAPON

The year 1949 marked an important stage in USSR defence strategy: the testing of an atomic weapon was, for the first time, officially announced by the government. Anti-Americanism spread, encouraged by the authorities: the Cold War began, and would last for decades.

In 1952, the Bolshevik Party became the Communist Party of the Soviet Union. The old guard (Molotov, Mikoyan, Voroshilov) was forced from power. On 5 March 1953, the very same day as the death of Stalin, a 'troika' comprising Malenkov, Voroshilov and Khrushchev assumed power. Stalin's terror came to an end: the major trials still being held were abandoned. Thanks to Marshal Zhukov, the Defence Minister, the dreaded Beria was arrested in the middle of a session of the Central Committee, and shot a few months later. This uncertain transitional period came to an end in September of that year, with the appointment of Khrushchev to the supreme post, that of First Secretary of the Central Committee.

His first decision was to take measures to improve the life of the kolkhoz inhabitants: the fate of the peasants remained one of the country's main problems. Malenkov, the instigator of the programme, also began to attack the bureaucracy which had been treating the people's needs with contempt. This didn't suit Khrushchev, who needed the apparatus to bolster his power: so he decided to pension Malenkov off.

Another crucial date was February 1956, which saw the XXth Party Congress. During a closed session, Khrushchev stupefied his audience by delivering his famous 'Report on the Personality Cult and its Consequences'. All the disastrous deviations from the correct way of building socialism were imputed to Stalin. Khrushchev drew up a balance sheet of Stalin's policies: on the credit side were the struggle against the opposition, the achievements of collectivization, industrialization and the victory over Hitler's Germany; on the debit side, the 'personality cult' that appeared when 'Stalin's character was starting to take a turn for the worse'. More than anything else, it was the sheer number of victims of the repression that left the congress members dumbstruck. The flower of society, the intellectual elite and thousands of innocent ordinary people had been destroyed.

But by knocking Stalin off his pedestal, Khrushchev shook people's faith in all leaders, himself included. The political system wasn't ready to tolerate an earthquake of such vehemence. In 1956, the crisis in Hungary and the crushing of the Budapest insurrection terrified the party apparatchiks, who feared that this movement might spread to the USSR itself: liberalization was put on hold. Khrushchev, who removed his 'rightist' adversaries and even his supporters (including Zhukov), assembled all power in his own hands. Political democratization was stopped, but the 'thaw' in intellectual life was to continue for another few years, awakening the romanticism of the revolutionary and post-revolutionary years, with their faith in the building of socialism.

Alas, the start of the 1960s was nothing but a series of economic failures. Khrushchev was feeling his way along: ideas that he held dear, such as the 'maize campaign' or the clearing of virgin land, led to catastrophic results. The peasantry was caught up in an ever-deeper crisis and abandoned the countryside, while shops emptied. The age-old traditions of the Russian heartland disappeared. The price of meat and butter rose; so did popular discontent. Demonstrations broke out in Novosherkassk, in the Donbass region, in Omsk and elsewhere: they were harshly repressed. The army itself had detested Khrushchev ever since 1955, the year in which the Warsaw Pact was created, but also the year when there was a massive reduction in the traditional arms budget in favour of nuclear weapons: all-in-all, the armed forces were reduced by almost two million soldiers. The Cuban crisis and the lack of rapport with China were the final blow to Khrushchev's prestige. But his decisive mistake was to threaten the interests of the nomenklatura and the Party apparatus. In October 1964 these latter plotted against him, and taking advantage of a time when he was on vacation, prepared for his deposition. Unceremoniously forced into retirement, he was replaced immediately by Leonid Brezhnev and Aleksei Kosygin.

The period that thus came to an end did, for all the errors committed by Stalin's successor, positively transform the Soviet Union in many domains: there was a rise in the standard of living, a massive house- and apartment-building programme, developments in science and technology, and a cultural thaw.

And above all, fanaticism and terror ceased to hold the country in their thrall.

THE STANDARDIZATION OF FIREARMS

In 1949, in recognition of my work, I was awarded the Stalin Prize. I learnt about it from the newspaper! I was overwhelmed when my eyes scanned the lines concerning me. On the same day, this prize was also awarded to Degtyarev and Simonov for their new firearms designs. I was told that people were astonished at how young I was, and in particular by the lowliness of my army grade. The Stalin Prize was a great honour, but also a veritable fortune: 150,000 roubles – a huge sum! With that, I could buy myself a dozen cars of the best make.

It was also in this year that I was demobilized. I was glad to get back to civilian life, but all the same, I didn't have any more spare time. You mustn't think that the task of a weapons designer ends when his invention moves on to the next stage of mass production. There's always new work to be done improving the manufacturing techniques, and you have to keep checking the quality of the weapons that leave the factory. In addition, you have to think about improving your models and creating new prototypes. You owe it to yourself to remain competitive in the race for progress.

Izhevsk had become the permanent place of residence of my family and myself. Katya had stopped working. She looked after everything at home: the children, the housework . . . She was very cheerful and sociable. With the simplest ingredients she managed to whip up delicious dinners to which our many friends were invited. Katya loved dancing, and she was very good at writing little satirical poems which made everyone laugh. Our house was full of fun and hospitality.

Right at the start of our life in Izhevsk, we occupied a single room in a shared flat. In addition, we didn't have any furniture to move in. In order to cobble together a mattress, my wife went to find hay in the nearby countryside. I can still see her, a radiant figure, coming back with her wagon laden with hay, so elegant in her feather hat.

We were a young couple. I didn't possess anything before I received the Stalin Prize; I was still just an ordinary soldier.

My wife wasn't particularly rich either. She and I both needed clothes. She was very pretty, and I wanted to give her outfits that would be worthy of her beauty. With the money from my bonus, we bought some fashionable clothes, and even a car. At that time, it was very difficult, since even if you had the necessary money, you also had to know the right people to get your hands on a car.

We left the motorbike factory, and the manufacture of the AK was transferred to Izhmash. I still work there these days, as chief designer of Kalashnikov weapons. I've always stayed a designer: I've never been the head of a company or manager, so I've never had any decision-making power. At that time, I was still completely unknown. Generally speaking, it was the manager of the factory who was at the forefront of things, not the inventors.

My activities were classified as 'Defence secrets', and I myself was obliged to maintain the utmost discretion. The city of Izhevsk, which numbered 300,000 inhabitants, was nonetheless itself kept 'secret'. It was a sort of 'forbidden zone'. Even these days, it is rare for outsiders to visit it. Officially, they need not only their Russian visa but also a special visa granting them entry to the city. The rules are gradually being relaxed, but even recently, my daughter encountered difficulties when she tried to find room in a city hotel for some French friends who didn't have this special visa.

*   *   *

Though I didn't have any patent for my invention, and never received a single kopek for arms sales, I did all the same pick up a significant salary, what in those days was called a 'personalized' salary. Our family lived rather well. We didn't have anything left over, but we never went short. As for me, I kept my grade as staff sergeant reservist. I stayed at this grade until the appearance, much later, of an American article which related that 'a mere Russian sergeant was arming all the countries in the Warsaw Pact' – this was the first time I'd been mentioned in the West! After this article appeared, the authorities started to promote me, as if coincidentally! Just as Yeltsin was appearing on the political scene, I'd already been hoisted up to the rank of colonel. I could have expected something better, but a decree of the Council of Ministers that forbade generals to be appointed in peacetime prevented it. Still, it was Yeltsin who, after the disintegration of the Soviet Union, took the decision to make an exception for me: I was appointed general.

At the Izhevsk factory where I continued to work, I had only a small team, while others had considerable groups of workers at their beck and call. I frequently requested a greater number of qualified personnel, but I never got what I wanted. I regret this, since I could very likely have come up with many other inventions in the weapons field, more quickly and with better working conditions.

Little by little, I became the deputy to the chief designer, and finally designer-in-chief myself. We had to work relentlessly, since we were continually competing with other weapons factories. Without false modesty, I have to say that in 50 years nobody has managed to outperform us. The reason is simple: it was the original idea of the AK-47 that was the best!

The simplicity and reliability of the AK-47 are found in all the other prototypes that our office designed, and that our factory produced. This is why it was difficult for our competitors to outstrip us. Even today, it is on the basis of my prototypes that the factory turns out guns, hunting rifles, etc., and naturally that gives me great pleasure.

These days, I'm no longer sworn to secrecy. I am in communication with people from all over the world, and I receive dozens of letters from abroad. Everyone thinks that I'm in charge of the factory. People don't realize that our system is quite different: apart from the designs of my weapons, I'm in charge of nothing. I do however have the honour of chairing the Union of Arms Manufacturers of Russia.

* * *

At the start of the 1950s, we came up against another problem, and a pretty significant one at that. A new objective had been assigned to Soviet arms designers: Stalin wanted all firearms to be standardized. At the time, the Soviet Army was equipped with three different types of firearms: my AK-47, Degtyarev's light machine gun and Simonov's semiautomatic rifle. The ammunition used was already of one standard model, but everything else was different. Each weapon comprised specific components, and even the loading varied from one model to the next: the light machine gun had a strip of 100 cartridges, the rifle had an immovable magazine of 10 cartridges, and my assault rifle a detachable magazine of 30 cartridges. It was obvious that significant benefits could be derived by standardizing the components.

So in 1954, the Main Artillery Directorate launched a new competition to devise standardized prototypes, which were to function with a new calibre. The conditions of the competition also laid it down that the weight of the weapons should be lessened and their aim improved. I worked on this problem on the basis of my model, as did Simonov and Degtyarev. I could have devised another prototype, but I didn't judge this to be necessary, since my AK-47 had already proved itself as a model of simplicity and reliability.

Standardization had always been the dream of all weapons designers. But nobody had yet turned the dream into a reality. It's not such a simple matter to combine the assault rifle and the light machine gun. Their construction rests on two different concepts. Not only that: the lifespan of an assault rifle is only half as long as that of a light machine gun. It is however possible to construct them on a common basis, which to my mind brings huge advantages: standardization enables one to cut back on size, and facilitates the use of firearms.

For example, imagine that in a combat situation, for some reason or another, one of the pieces of your weapon stops working: you can then replace this with a piece from another weapon. If you run out of ammunition, the same is true: you can then go and see the colleague in charge of light machine guns and ask him for what you need.

I can't explain why, apart from Russia, no one has gone down this route, with the exception of those countries that base their automatic weapons on the Kalashnikov, such as Israel. A soldier who can handle an assault rifle will also be able to use a light machine gun without any difficulty. All its actions and all its movements are the same.

*   *   *

When it came to standardization, one of the greatest difficulties lay in the way the weapons were loaded. The light machine gun had a feed strip of 100 cartridges: my model was supposed, in accordance with the conditions imposed by the competition, to have many fewer. Eventually I made a round metallic magazine that could contain 75 cartridges. It was successfully tested in the factory, and turned out to be strong and reliable. Firing in 'unstable' positions was improved by introducing a new muzzle brake. All the pieces that could be dismantled were designed in such a way that they were interchangeable between one firearm and another.

My assault rifle and my light machine gun were made much lighter, and their aim improved. I also replaced the bayonet by a knife. It was very effective. With this knife, placed at the end of the barrel and easy to unfix, you could for instance cut through barbed wire, even when it was electrified.

The competition trials started in our good old Polygon in the environs of Moscow. They proceeded in the usual way: several rounds, with some entries being eliminatied each time, and a single victor. In the last round, I was still in the running and found myself up against the engineer Korobov, from the Tula factory. Korobov had devised some good assault rifles and light machine guns. Everyone was plumping for him, but in the end I was the winner!

The work carried out during this period was very well described by Malimon:

> Work to standardize weapons occupied most of the research laboratories in 1955 and 1956. As well as G. A. Korobov and A. S. Konstantinov, who had anticipated the request, the following participated in the competition: M. T. Kalashnikov, S. G. Simonov, V. A. Degtyarev and G. S. Garanin.
>
> Shortly after the work and the testing began, those responsible for setting the norms lowered the intended life-span of an assault rifle by a third, vis-à-vis the AK-47, taken as the standard. The weight stipulation was also relaxed: the weapon could now weigh 3.1 kg instead of 2.8 kg.
>
> All the models proposed succeeded in the preliminary trials, with the exception of Simonov's assault rifle. The models put forward by Kalashnikov, based on the AK-47, also underwent several trials on the Polygon. But after all these experiments, the authorities decided, at the end of 1955, simply to modernize the existing AK-47.
>
> At the end of 1956, several weapons research laboratories presented their models for assault rifles and light machine guns at the new competition organized by the Polygon.
>
> After a few preliminary trials, Kalashnikov's new assault rifle was perfected. It included a breechblock shutter constructed all in one piece, a visor and a butt fixing

similar to those of the existing AK, and it was rid of the components that had been borrowed from the automatic rifle and that handicapped its performance. Construction by stamping of the breechblock unit, the main innovation of the modernized AK, made it possible for its weight to be perceptibly reduced and to diminish the quantity of metal used.

And only Kalashnikov's weapon showed itself able to satisfy entirely the demands for reliability in difficult conditions (dust and rain). The conclusion of the competition jury was that it was the most promising. The models submitted by Korobov and Konstantinov, technically superior to the AK, were given honourable marks. And the most accomplished, Korobov's, was selected for later phases of development, together with Kalashnikov's model.

Thus my AKM assault rifle ('M' for 'modernized') and my RPK light machine gun ('RPK' for 'Kalashnikov light machine gun') were chosen for use in the army in preference to all the others.

My assault rifle was a perfectly good substitute, in fact, for Simonov's rifle, whose best points it combined with its own qualities. The advent of the AKM thus entailed a halt in the production of Simonov rifles.

Now, in place of three models of firearms, there were only two: the AKM and the RPK, which used the same 7.62-calibre ammunition. In addition, their essential components were totally interchangeable, which made them easier for the army to use and meant that their production was more cost-effective.

From then on, the whole Soviet army was equipped solely with weapons that I had designed – Kalashnikov weapons! And this was true throughout the Soviet period.

*   *   *

My success in weapons standardization earned me the title of 'Hero of Socialist Labour', which the government gave me in 1958 for 'reinforcing the power of the state'.

This standardization required two years of intense and relentless daily labour. The 'brains' in our factory was a group of young designers. My closest collaborators, Krupin, Pushin, Kriakushin and Kharkov, were still under 30. I was the oldest at the time – 29. Alas, Pushin died prematurely, probably as a result of the nervous stress associated with our work.

Krupin was the last of my close collaborators to remain alive. He was assassinated in autumn 2002, while returning from our Izhmash factory, by a gang of young delinquents. I felt a profound sense of injustice when I learned that this extraordinary man, who had survived the war and dedicated his whole life to the future of our country, had just been beaten to death by young men who were supposed to represent precisely this future. It is terrifying to see how many young people don't have any jobs, don't pick up any education, aren't interested in anything, take drugs, and in fact just ruin their lives – as well as the lives of others.

When I think that we practically never took any holidays, that we spent Sundays and days off together, at each other's homes, exchanging our ideas about our current projects . . . We had really cramped accommodation; this never stopped us from getting together and having a good time. At that time, Soviet youth was full of enthusiasm, and delinquency barely existed. Those years were certainly the happiest in our lives.

ONE MORE STEP

Once standardization had been achieved, another workshop was opened, for a second stage in the development of

firearms: this involved devising a unique machine gun, able
to replace all the other machine guns found in the army. It
was a difficult mission, since the new weapon would have to
combine all the qualities of pre-existing machine guns (able
to be operated from a tank, a troop transporter, on a gun car-
riage, and as a heavy machine gun).

To begin with, it was the unique machine gun devised by
Nikitin, from the Tula weapons factory, that produced the
best results. But his weapon had one drawback that he could
not correct: once it had been immersed in water, it worked
much less well. When it became clear that Nikitin couldn't
correct this drawback, the military personnel in charge of
this project turned to me.

At that time, I still had a small team of designers; we were
working on the standardization of weapons and the use of a
bullet of a new calibre. Although I hadn't turned 40, I was
still the oldest member of the team. And an exceptional team
it was: the engineers and workers were all very talented, and
worked with great fervour.

The essential mechanisms of the new machine gun were
meant to be analogous to those of my other models. Very
careful thought had to be taken over the new components to
be introduced. But there was also a collective challenge: to
demonstrate our capacity and the quality of our work
by beating the Tula design team! And yet in just a few
months, a ridiculously short period, we built our machine
gun.

My deputies carried out trials on different sites, in varying
climatic conditions. Our machine gun, which behaved very
well in Russia, demonstrated several weaknesses in the hot,
sandy terrain of Uzbekistan, in Samarkand. The solutions to
the problems were simple, but extremely difficult to apply –
as so often in life! For instance, in order to resolve the
problem of how to use the weapon in conditions of great

heat, we had to change the skin of the barrel, covering it with chrome. For this, I went to Samarkand, together with Krupin.

On my return, I noticed that my factory colleagues were behaving very strangely. Then I read an abominable article about myself in the factory newspaper, where they wrote about the 'personality cult' and its disastrous consequences! This injustice made me literally ill. I started to suffer from cardiac arrhythmia. In spite of that, I continued with my trials on the standardized machine gun.

This was the period during which the personality cult inherited from Stalin was being attacked everywhere. The government called for it to be denounced wherever it could be found, even within families! It started to assume quite exaggerated proportions. According to the Party's decision, the personality cult wasn't restricted to Stalin: it also affected several people in authority on a local scale, and these people needed to be sought out and punished.

Apparently, people had been instructed to speak at our factory meetings. And these people declared that there was in our midst a personality cult of Kalashnikov!

People are herd-like. Everyone applauded, happy to see me being lambasted. Several immediately wrote to the newspapers to say that I treated others with contempt, disdained their talents, and so on.

My view of things darkened. I was so painfully affected by the attacks levelled at me that I felt a need to express my feelings in a poem that I wrote just after the Party meeting at which I had been slandered:

> *I've weighed up everything scrupulously,*
> *In life I've lost all support,*
> *My heart no longer beats properly,*
> *My whole body's numb and taut.*

They tell me the sledge is outside
To take me to the cemetery
I'm like a man dead and buried
Everything is collapsing around me.

This persecution lasted for several months, but fortunately, at a later meeting of the factory's Communist Party, the wind changed. According to a new decision of the Central Committee, the personality cult could be applied only to Stalin.

I was rehabilitated. The Party Secretary described me in quite different terms. He even rebuked a designer who'd had been particularly vocal in dragging me through the mud. This was a very hard period for me; in fact, I've never altogether forgiven some of my colleagues for their hostile attitude towards me, and their unjust remarks. But all I could do was carry on working with them. This was the only period in my life when I thought of giving it all up.

Still, I decided to swallow my resentment and all my feelings of anger, and to close the door on this unhappy episode, so as to dedicate myself completely to my plans for a standardized machine gun.

It was only in 1961 that the Soviet Army adopted my unique PK machine gun, with all its variants. This was the second 'wave' of firearms standardization. A few years later, we learnt that our work had been put forward as a candidate for the Lenin Prize. I eventually received it in 1964, with a group of designers who worked with me. This was one of the most important state distinctions, granted for outstanding achievements in different areas (science, technology, literature, art . . .). Set up in 1925, after the death of Lenin, it hadn't been awarded to anyone between 1935 and 1957, during which time it was replaced by the Stalin Prize: subsequently, in 1966, this was replaced by the State Prize.

My collaborators and I received, together with a prize, a bonus of 7,500 roubles, a far from negligible sum at the time, though in the final analysis it was rather symbolic as it had to be shared out between eight people. I personally received 2,500 roubles: with that amount, I couldn't even buy half a car. Katya and I blew this small fortune together, at a big party organized by our friends.

I was summoned to Moscow to receive the prize. I had to bring my latest designs with me to present to the members of the jury. One of these, General Blagonravov, was an old acquaintance: I'd met him in Samarkand, right at the start of my professional activities as a designer. It was he who had to some extent launched me on my career by writing a letter to a senior civil servant at the Defence Ministry, in which he expressed a very favourable opinion about my work. He'd been the first to believe in my future as a designer. At that time, in 1942, he asked the minister to give me the means to get an education and to develop my capabilities.

General Blagonravov recognized me when I started to speak in front of the jury, and he gave me a smile of complicity. After my presentation, he came to see me: 'So, I'm the godfather of everything you've done, am I?' He seemed very moved and he gave me a warm embrace.

* * *

I then launched into a new project – adapting my weapons to a reduced calibre of ammunition. During the Vietnam War, the Americans adopted a small calibre: 5.56 mm. I was rather hostile to a reduced calibre being used by us. Even now, I am still convinced that the 7.62 calibre is the best. But arms manufacturers abroad were already tackling the question, so I too became involved in it.

I divided my collaborators into several sub-groups. We set up innumerable trials. A smaller calibre didn't simply involve changing the barrel: it was a real technical challenge. However odd it may appear, the presence of water in the barrel made the weapon unserviceable when ammunition of a smaller calibre was used.

Not without difficulty, we finally managed to build a reliable barrel. To obtain the requisite precision of aim, we had to design special mechanisms for the barrel mouth. The alterations led to the weapon being lighter and more efficient in combat. Trials demonstrated that the basic principle of the AKM assault rifle easily lent itself to completely workable variants. Given the good results from the experiments carried out with the new ammunition, *all* my weapons had to be modified so they could be adapted to reduced-calibre cartridges.

This time, it was the team from the city of Kovrov that we found to be our fiercest competitors, while usually our most redoubtable rivals were the Tula designers. Several times over, my designs ended up in the finals of the competition, against those from the Tula factory. And even when we won, they were always worthy opponents. By some quirk of fate, it was the Technical Institute of Tula that decided, in 1971, to award me a doctorate in technical sciences, without passing through the usual stages. This title was awarded me for my work as a whole. It was considered that I'd opened up a new stage in the development of firearms, and this also meant I was awarded my second title of 'Hero of Socialist Labour' in 1976. As you can see, the Soviet Government was never stingy about lavishing titles and decorations on me.

On one occasion, this last distinction was of considerable practical help to me. When Ustinov,[1] the Defence Minister, announced the news to me, I was doubled over with cramp and experiencing searing pains on my left side and down my back: it was an attack of nephritic colic. As I have a phobia about injections and people in white coats, I absolutely refused to go to hospital. My wife went in my place to consult the doctors.

Three hours after Ustinov's telephone call, I managed (without any medical help) to pass the kidney stone that had been causing my problems. A double hero owed it to himself to overcome his bodily weaknesses!

* * *

At the start of the 1960s, in the Khrushchev era, it was decided to close down the Shurovo Polygon. I thought this decision was particularly unfair, since this testing ground was essential for building good firearms. It was all scrapped, including the equipment from the labs. I consider it to have been a severe blow to the development of Russian firearms. In addition, after the suppression of the site, the best engineers and technicians were scattered to the four corners of the country.

This place played a special role in my life. I worked there during and after the war; much later, I was still undertaking assignments there. The workshops were modern, and very well equipped. The best engineers and designers from all over the USSR came here to test out their weapons. Some engineers were present all year round. They constituted the 'brains' of the Polygon, which depended on the army. The site was in the middle of the forests and constituted a small military town all by itself, with all the necessary services: the headquarters, the apartment blocks where the officers' families lived, and so on. These were communal apartments, shared by several families. There were also hostels for bachelors and a hotel – always crammed – for those assigned there for periods of work.

Not only that: it was here that I had met the woman who was to become my wife, Katya Moiseyeva. So this place was all the dearer to me.

At that time, entire swathes of the army suffered from Nikita Khrushchev's 'all-nuclear' policy: the government allocated much less money to anything involving conventional weapons. When Khrushchev came to power, it was decided to reduce the production of firearms, and employees started to leave the factory. All the same, I continued to suggest improvements on my assault rifle and to work on new prototypes.

I feel sad for Russia, which doesn't always appreciate the quality of its designers the way it should. In any other country, when a weapon is furnished with a new component or any kind of innovation, people describe it as a 'new prototype'. But not in Russia. I've lost count of my original innovations that deserved to be developed, and that were just scrapped, melted down. It was so stupid not to keep them! But with us this was, unfortunately, the rule: the models that weren't going to be put into mass manufacture were eliminated. In my team, there was a qualified worker assigned to melting down my innovations. I invented, he destroyed, without leaving a trace. We each had our own job to do! Once, I asked him, 'Don't you ever get fed up of doing it?'

'You just need to come up with fewer ideas. That'll mean less work for me!'

In this way, just so that a few kilos of steel could be recycled, the history of weapons was made immeasurably poorer.

*   *   *

Every nation should respect its army. This is no longer the case in Russia today. I accuse the politicians of dragging the army into internal conflicts, and I am sad to see the media forever attacking this institution. They've also started laying into the great generals of bygone days, such as Zhukov – they say his role wasn't at all as significant as people believed. They are so wrong!

A world without wars and without weapons is a utopian ideal, but we should do all in our power to try and attain that ideal. Will we ever be able to maintain and manage peace without weapons? I very much doubt it. The weapon that I created and that bears my name lives its own life, independent of my life and my desires. Of course, when I see Bin Laden on television with his Kalashnikov, I'm disgusted, but what can I do about it? Terrorists aren't stupid: they too choose the most reliable weapons!

Ever since the 1950s, my assault weapons have been in circulation in the army. Every time I'm invited to military sites, the soldiers are eager to express their gratitude to me. They show their thanks because I've given them a weapon that won't let them down.

5

'HE WAS A GOD;

HE MIGHT RISE AGAIN'

In 1950, Kalashnikov, to his great surprise, was put forward as a deputy to the Supreme Soviet of the USSR: this made it possible for him to see (from afar) Stalin and other dignitaries and celebrities of the country. He would have a seat in the Supreme Soviet, apart from a gap of 10 years, until this institution disappeared in 1988.

According to the 1936 Constitution, the Supreme Soviet represented the highest rung of power. In fact, the important questions were dealt with by the Party, which in practice left the Soviet with a merely decorative role. During Stalin's lifetime, the agenda was drawn up by the Guide himself, and the deputies voted unanimously for the ukases and the budgets. This didn't exclude the deputies from playing a positive role at the local level, and this was the case for Kalashnikov: he would use his celebrity to do what he could for his electors.

Then came Khrushchev, who tried to de-Stalinize the country and its institutions. Kalashnikov was not re-elected in 1954.

He returned to the Supreme Soviet only in 1966, during Brezh-
nev's 'thaw'.

The reign of Leonid Brezhnev (from 1964 to 1982) was a time
of doublespeak, political intrigue, the emergence of a 'black
market' and the rise of the gerontocracy. Thanks to his bon-
homie and his art of pleasing everybody, Brezhnev created a
circle of loyal supporters around him. In spite of his attempts
at economic reform, the USSR remained in thrall to the model
of extensive development: natural resources were wasted, the
country was hit by ecological disasters and massive amounts
of money were invested on the military-industrial complex and
space projects.

The Brezhnev era has passed into history as a period of
'stagnation': national revenue and production peaked out,
and bureaucracy flourished. Science and technology marked
time. Manual rather than mechanized labour remained the
norm.

The political climate hardened, and intellectuals were muz-
zled. Those who were later called 'dissidents' mobilized to
defend human rights. They were severely repressed (Daniel,
Sinyavksy, Ginzburg), placed under house arrest (Sakharov),
interned in psychiatric clinics (General Grigoryenko) or exiled
(Solzhenitsyn, Brodsky and many others). Around 1980, some
500 leaders of the dissident movement were behind bars.

The army, to which the government devoted considerable
time and money, overtook that of the United States. But a few
years before his death, Brezhnev committed a fatal error: in
December 1979, Soviet troops entered Afghanistan.

Brezhnev bequeathed this fateful inheritance to his succes-
sors, in particular Mikhail Gorbachev, who would try from 1985
onwards to 'reconstruct' (cf. the Russian word 'perestroika')
the USSR on a new basis.

With perestroika, the stagnation experienced under
Brezhnev gave way to a new flood of initiatives, both individual

and collective. 'Glasnost' (openness, transparency) offered Russia a degree of freedom it had never known. An adept at compromise, Gorbachev, who failed to free himself from the heavy hand of the Party apparatus, was forced into taking contradictory decisions. He came up against new Russian 'democrats' such as the historian Yuri Afanasiev, who denounced the 'Stalino-Brezhnevite' Supreme Soviet.

By 1989, Gorbachev had lost his credibility, and then his grip of political events, which teetered out of control. The economic crisis, aggravated by the Party apparatus, which dragged its feet, was further complicated by inter-ethnic conflict which broke out in several Soviet republics. The power of Russia itself rose, to the detriment of federal authority.

The putsch of August 1991, carried out by people nostalgic for the old regime, was the final blow for the USSR. From now on, real power was held by Boris Yeltsin, the ebullient President of Russia, who stripped Gorbachev of all his prerogatives and, aided and abetted by his opposite numbers from the Ukraine and Byelorussia, paved the way for the dissolution of the Soviet Union. This disappeared formally in December 1991, with the resignation of Gorbachev.

DAILY LIFE OF A DEPUTY IN THE SUPREME SOVIET

I was elected deputy in 1950, shortly after receiving the Stalin Prize. I was still only 30. Apart from my factory colleagues, I knew nobody and nobody knew me. So when I was told that I'd been selected as a candidate to the post of deputy, I was flabbergasted!

Deputies to the Supreme Soviet of the USSR were elected for four years and represented a given region. The number of deputies per region depended on the number of inhabitants. For the region of Udmurtia alone, where I came from, there were a good dozen or so deputies. Altogether, I was elected six times: from 1950 to 1954, then from 1966 to 1988.

All citizens were eligible, whatever their social conditions, professions or nationalities. It was possible to combine the function of deputy with another job. The aim of parliamentary sessions was to discuss the country's budget, or new laws, and to vote for them. The bills were prepared in advance by special commissions; for example, I was a permanent member of the budgetary commission.

During the sessions of the Supreme Soviet, deputies would go to Moscow for a week, no longer. But the members of the commissions came together a month before the start of the plenary sessions. The deputies who were not from Moscow and had no accommodation in the capital stayed at the Hotel Moskva – later on, the Hotel Rossiya came to be preferred. The state paid for travel and lodging, but we paid for food and entertainment ourselves.

The candidatures of the deputies were carefully chosen by the authorities of republics or regions: one deputy per constituency. This produced a list of 'candidates' that was published in the newspapers and announced on the radio. The candidates could then begin to meet their electors. At each meeting, the latter voiced their needs. On this basis, a programme was drawn up which the candidate was to carry out during the four years of his or her term of office. It was no picnic, but a difficult task and a great responsibility towards one's electors.

The first time I came to take part in a meeting of deputies to the Supreme Soviet in Moscow, I was in a blue funk when I came through the Spassky Gate, one of the entries to the Kremlin. The guards checked all those coming in, and scrutinized every face. I thought they were going to arrest me – it was impossible the Kremlin could be unaware of my past as an 'escapee'. Nevertheless, I came in and out through the Spassky Gate without let or hindrance during my 30 years' term of office.

When I became a deputy, I still wasn't a member of the Party. I only joined it in 1953. I was still afraid people might make enquiries into my past, and find out what I'd kept quiet for all those years. It was only when I received the Stalin Prize that the managers of my factory realized that I wasn't even a member of the Communist Party. It was explained to me that 'decent' people owed it to themselves to be in the Party. I had to join without delay.

My first term of office as a deputy was particularly important for me. Until then, I'd only ever worked on my weapons: nothing else existed for me. Here I really learned about the life of my country, especially via the stories told to me by the people who came to see me.

I had to go to Moscow two or three times a year to attend the meetings of the Supreme Soviet and the preparations beforehand. I took my duties very seriously, and felt truly honoured by my title and by that small portion of responsibility that falls on a man of state. In those days, the situation of a deputy brought you neither privilege nor celebrity, and didn't require any particular lifestyle. In general, you were chosen for your performance at work, and because you'd shown your mettle. Among the deputies, there were Heroes of the Soviet Union, Heroes of Socialist Labour, marshals and generals, cosmonauts and scientists, but also artists, sportsmen and women, workers and peasants. These days, one might well be a bit sceptical at this type of 'election', where you are appointed in an authoritarian way. But at the time, this wasn't considered as a violation of liberties.

Thanks to my new responsibilities, I was fortunate to meet people who counted among the most intelligent in the country: for example, the poet Rasul Gamzatov, the cosmonaut Yuri Gagarin, the famous writer Mikhail Sholokhov (author of *Quiet Flows the Don*, my favourite novel) and the celebrated ophthalmologist and surgeon Federov. I was very often tempted to go up to Sholokhov and make his acquaintance, but I never dared. Among the deputies, you didn't find any 'lobbyists', as crooked politicians are known these days. I honestly think that the authorities did keep themselves at arm's length from the underworld and its shady dealings. Nowadays, the elector really can choose which deputy to elect, but who's he going to choose: a thief who has money to fund his electoral campaign? or a demagogue who plays on nationalist sentiments?

For my part, I am proud of the time I spent as a deputy, of all those years spent in the service of my country.

Before my first election, there was a semblance of an electoral campaign. The constituency for which I was a candidate included three rural zones and an urban zone. I often had to travel about to see my electors.

The roads in the Izhevsk region were in a dreadful condition. Much later, I took advantage of the visit of one of the most powerful secretaries in the Central Committee, Dmitri Ustinov, who had come to Izhevsk to see the weapons factories, to complain about the dilapidated condition of the road network in our region. Ustinov, whom I knew well, had been at the head of the entire military industry in the Soviet Union during the war. He promised to get me a 4 × 4 vehicle. This was my dream. Shortly afterwards, I received a telegram: 'Drop by at the car factory to buy your car.' With this vehicle, I certainly covered many kilometres, criss-crossing the region!

With my election, a new period in my life began. The electors had demonstrated their trust in me; I was proud of this, and fully resolved to do everything in my power to improve their living conditions.

When I arrived in Izhevsk, there wasn't a single square metre of tarmac. It was more of a small town than a town. In my capacity as deputy, I drew up a request for roadworks addressed to the Deputy President of the Soviet of Ministers. This request concerned the construction of a factory to produce tarmac. These days, people say that deputies did nothing for their electors, or for the good of the country. I would dispute that. Just like me, they did everything in their power to resolve the problems of their electors, whose lives were often not all that easy.

However odd this might seem, I gave my first speech as a deputy in a church. In a town within my constituency, not far from Izhevsk, all the political meetings were held in a church! This building was in such a tumbledown state that it was dangerous for the people who always turned up in considerable numbers to my meetings. At this time, the government had provisionally stopped putting up new public buildings. Nonetheless, by dint of persevering, I managed to persuade them to build a Palace of Culture near Izhevsk. One day, shortly after the building had been finished, I pointed out to the manager that the palace was surrounded by a stretch of wasteland overrun by wild grass. After all the efforts I'd put into getting it built, I was outraged: they could have taken a bit better care of the environs.

When I returned in the winter for a meeting, there were some magnificent flowers growing in front of the entrance! To begin with, I was really amazed and delighted, as I thought it was some extremely rare species of flower able to grow in the snow. I complimented the manager, who started to smile and looked very pleased with himself. As I left, I tried to tear off a petal, and the whole plant came out! The flowers were artificial. I pretended not to have noticed; indeed, I even asked the manager to obtain some seeds of those magnificent flowers for me, and he had the cheek to promise that he'd send some to me at the next opportunity!

There were few deputies who were re-elected for a second term of office: mainly the directors of regions or republics, or people who were particularly popular with the electors. I'm not going to put on any false modesty: my several re-elections could be explained by the fact that the celebrity of my name opened the doors to the offices of great personages, which made it so much easier to get problems solved. And there was no lack of problems, especially out in the provinces. And it was thanks to my fame that I was able to play a part in the development of not only my constituency, but also our entire little republic of Udmurtia, of which Izhevsk is the capital. I can pride myself on certain concrete achievements in this town. I contributed to the building of roads, hospitals, schools; I obtained credits for a music school to be built right next door to my home.

*   *   *

All these activities often led us to neglect our private lives.

My wife Katya and my children were proud of me, but I was – even more often than previously – away from home, since there were not just my trips to the Polygon but also my tours as a deputy. Electors would occasionally come to see me directly in our little flat. I would hold improvised meetings in one of our two rooms. My wife took good care to close the doors, telling the children not to make any noise: they could only play in the kitchen or the yard.

Several times, I was elected as a member of the commission that decided on how the budget was to be shared out right across the Soviet Union. During the month that followed a session, on our return from Moscow, we would go to see the workers in the firms in our constituencies and explain the measures adopted. Between two meetings of the

Supreme Soviet, we would receive the electors and the representatives of the firms. We listened to their problems and tried to solve them. The people who came were all very different. Often they were women who had lost their husbands in the war; they had few resources and came asking for help. They had to be given work or accommodation.

Sometimes the most incredible things would happen to me, I would receive the weirdest visits: harebrained inventors would arrive with their drawings, intent on telling me of their discoveries, and complaining that nobody understood them. I also remember one strange visitor. In 1953, the year of Stalin's death, an amnesty was declared: among the crowd of those set free there were thieves and other delinquents. One day, a tall, handsome young man came ringing at my door. He showed me his release papers, and told me he'd been obliged to carry out an armed raid on a shop because his father, wounded in the war, needed medicine. He wanted to work in our factory, and asked for some clothes. Because my wife and I took a liking to him, we gave him some shirts and a suit that were all too big for me. A few days later, my wife bumped into him at the market; he was selling clothes, including mine! He was a 'professional' salesman!

BEHIND THE WALLS OF THE KREMLIN

The first time I saw Stalin at a meeting, I was filled with awe. I remember with perfect clarity the way he came into the great hall in which we had gathered. Stalin was wearing his eternal semi-military suit. He sat in his place, the same one as ever, in the midst of a total silence. And then there was thunderous outbreak of applause that lasted an eternity, since nobody wanted to be the first to stop! After several minutes, Stalin gestured with his hand, asking for quiet in the assembly. All at once, you could have heard a pin drop.

I never drew any connection between the tragedy that had struck our family and the person of Stalin. I thought the fault lay with little local bureaucrats. In my view, they were the ones really guilty for the deportation of our family to Siberia and my brother's exile to the Gulag. As for Stalin, he was beyond suspicion as far as I was concerned. We'd been brought up with the idea that the Soviet victory in the Second World War was due to him. He was almost closer to us than our own parents; it's difficult to imagine it these days. We thought that it was thanks to Stalin that we'd been able to build socialism. We were grateful to him for free health and education. People were now all equal, and that too was thanks to him. On the radio, they never stopped telling us about our chief, the 'Little Father of the People'. And from dawn to dusk they sang songs to the glory of Comrade Stalin. When the newspapers related the misdeeds of the 'enemies of the people', those saboteurs of the revolution, or of the doctors who wanted to kill Stalin, we thought they were real bastards. People demanded the death penalty for those traitors!

The poet Mikhail Isakovsky[1] wrote these lines after the death of Stalin: they expressed what we were all feeling:

> *Our faith in you, Comrade Stalin,*
> *was immense,*
> *A hundred times greater and more intense*
> *Than all our most private feelings.*

When Stalin was buried, the whole population wept. We felt that life couldn't go on without him. Fear of the future gripped our hearts.

I saw Stalin at the meetings of the Supreme Soviet in 1950, 1951 and 1952. He spoke very rarely. Each of his appearances was the occasion for triumphal acclaim. During the session, he spoke to nobody in particular. He attended the morning's meetings for the full four hours, always dressed in the same strict, severe fashion, but in the afternoons his place was empty. I never saw him laugh, and very rarely did a fleeting smile light up his face. He gave the impression of being preoccupied. In the meetings that he chaired in person, an iron discipline reigned. The thought of chatting to their neighbours never even crossed the deputies' minds.

After Stalin's death, the atmosphere changed completely. The deputies talked to one another freely, and discussed everything, except politics: they rarely listened very closely to what the speakers were saying. I remember one incident that could never possibly have happened during Stalin's lifetime. The famous cosmonaut Valentina Tereshkova,[2] who was sitting in front of me, lost a button. It rolled to the ground, and I bent down to pick it up. In Stalin's day, the button would have continued on its way without anyone daring to notice it! Indeed, I'm sure that Tereshkova would never have dared to lose it.

I consider Stalin as one of the great national leaders of the twentieth century, and as a great army leader. On the tank I drove during the war was written the motto 'For the Motherland, for Stalin'. That shows how much we believed in him. I think that Khrushchev's revelations during the XXth Party Congress stemmed from a personal vendetta. Perhaps he'd been offended by Stalin, or perhaps he wanted to belittle the grandeur and the merits of our 'Guide', which cast his own in the shade. Even now, I am convinced that those declarations pleased very few people. I am happy to admit that the repression carried out by the KGB in the 1930s was of an unacceptable cruelty that struck at soldiers, scientists and peasants. Many people were punished without proof. It's difficult to understand. No doubt the dictatorship of the proletariat seemed the only way to keep and reinforce power, in a country surrounded by capitalist powers, even after 20 years of Soviet might. During the war, we believed in Stalin as much as in God. We were ready to lay down our lives for the motherland and for him. The motto written on our tank was in any case a cult slogan during the war. The soldiers would go into battle and die with those words on their lips. As the poet Tvardovsky put it: 'He was a god, he might rise again.' Stalinism was really a faith, the faith that animated the heroes of the Soviet Union, such as Matrosov, who sacrificed his own life by flinging himself onto a German cannon to protect his comrades, or Zoya Kosmodemyanskaya, martyred by the fascists, and so many others.

In any case, I'm sure that he was an extraordinary and highly intelligent man. All those who had any dealings with him attest that he was endowed with an exceptional memory, never forgetting anything, not even the surname and first name of people he had met only once. I never knew him personally, and I regret this. They say that before awarding me the Stalin Prize, he kept my AK-47 on his desk for several days.

Later on, Khrushchev obliged the holders of the Stalin Prize to give back their certificates and medals. In exchange, they received what was called the 'State Prize'. I regret that I complied. What's the point of falsifying history?

* * *

Miraculously, our Polygon was spared from the so-called 'Stalinist purges'. We were young and enthusiastic, and the only thought we had in our heads was the invention of new weapons for the defence of our motherland. We had neither the time nor any desire to get involved in intrigues and denunciations.

We had a great deal of respect for Bulba, the director of the Polygon, and his deputy, Lieutenant-Colonel Nikolai Okhotnikov. The latter's destiny is quite instructive. Before the Revolution, his father was at the head of the nobility of a great region; his brother, having served in the White Army of Wrangel, had to leave Russia. Someone decided to mention the 'dubious' past of his family to the authorities. Okhotnikov was immediately expelled from the ranks of the Red Army. But he was allowed to stay on at the Polygon, and he tried by every means at his disposal to repair the injustice that had been done to him, even going so far as to write to Stalin himself. Bulba, with insane bravery, dared to take up the cudgels in defence of his deputy – and won! Not only was Okhotnikov given back his post, but two years later he was promoted.

* * *

The leaders of the USSR who succeeded Stalin didn't impress me much. Khrushchev was a remarkable orator whose talents were recognized by all the deputies. He loved to speak. When he was criticizing something or someone, he did it in rather a brutal manner. He loved to pat himself on the back and make incredible promises. Often he was in a good mood, affable and playful in the evening gatherings organized by the government at the Kremlin. But I never had any opportunity to talk to him face-to-face.

Khrushchev considered firearms as antiques whose time had come and gone. He staked everything on missiles, especially intercontinental missiles, considering that they were essential to Russia's military power.

As for Brezhnev, I did meet him in person, on several occasions. He came to see me at our factory in Izhevsk. He wasn't yet 50 when I made his acquaintance; nor was he yet General Secretary of the Party (the 'real' boss of the USSR), but President of the Presidium of the Supreme Soviet. He tried out our new designs of machine and sub-machine guns personally. He was an excellent marksman, full of initiative and very energetic. He made a lot of promises to one's face, but these often remained a dead letter.

When Brezhnev came to Izhevsk, I again tried to talk to him in person about plans for a centre for weapons engineers that could replace the famous Polygon in the environs of Moscow that had been so inopportunely demolished. I wanted this centre to be built next to our factory. While I was talking to him, Brezhnev was handling different prototypes, paying particular attention to the knife bayonets. I started to wonder, with some vexation, whether his advisers had told him that the essential merits of my weapons were to be found elsewhere. Then everything became clear when Brezhnev leaned towards me and whispered in my ear, 'Might it be possible to steal this knife from you?' I made a vague gesture in reply: far from dissuading him, it bolstered his intention of taking it away for good. I gave it to him with the consent of the factory manager. He seemed ecstatic: he thought the knife would come in handy when he went hunting.

'I'll organize a really big party for your birthday', he suggested.

'Thanks for the party, but don't bother. What I really *would* like would be for this centre for engineers to be built.'

'It will be built, don't you worry.'

This episode made us think about the types of presents that could be given to the senior functionaries who came to visit the factory. We settled on a hunting knife that had several functions: it could serve as a bottle-opener (important for hunting!), as a screwdriver and as a very sturdy file, capable of sawing into wood and even metal. The first knife to leave the factory was naturally meant to go to Leonid Brezhnev, on whom the fate of the engineers' centre depended. On this knife were engraved four letters: LBMK, meaning 'for Leonid Brezhnev, from Mikhail Kalashnikov'.

But it was written that this knife was to meet with another destiny.

In spring 1964, while I was briefly staying in Moscow, someone told me, 'Marshal Voronov would like you to call by'. And he slipped me his telephone number. I suddenly felt ashamed: how could I have failed to think of it myself? I should have dropped by to thank him long ago. It all suddenly came back to me: his private train wagon, our dinner together, his encouragements – 'I'm sure that you're the man who will manage to standardize Soviet weapons', he'd told me.

On the telephone, his voice was mocking: 'When you were a sergeant, you used to come and see me. Now you're a "hero", you've forgotten the old marshal.' He invited me round to see him that very same day. I had only a few hours in which to find a present for him. The idea occurred to me that I could give him the same knife that I myself had made for Brezhnev.

This knife, that I now intended for Voronov, had to be hastily modified: *his* initials had to appear on it. In the end, he was delighted at the result: the knife threw him into raptures. He congratulated me: 'Don't forget that you're a famous designer now. I knew it would happen. I'm happy for you. It's not for nothing that I kept your photo with the autograph!'

Later on, Brezhnev received his knife too, but he didn't keep his promise: the centre was never built.

As for Gorbachev, in all the greetings cards he sent me, he declared himself convinced that the Soviet people's lives would get better and better if they supported his idea of perestroika, the reconstruction of society and state. Under his leadership, we did indeed reconstruct the country, passing from socialism to democracy with a 'new Russian' – or nouveau riche – flavour.

Gorbachev decorated me with the medal of honour of machine designers. He never came to Izhevsk, but on my birthday he always sent me congratulatory telegrams. That doesn't stop me hating him deeply for all the damage he did to our country by allowing the fall of the Soviet Union. But the one who really led the country to its ruin was his successor, Yeltsin. I always thought he looked self-satisfied and haughty; he spoke slowly and dragged out his words.

Yeltsin decorated me with a medal on which is represented a two-headed eagle. On my jacket, this eagle sits next to the two stars of the Hero of Socialist Labour, the Order of Lenin, the Order of Saint Andrew and the others – I've surely been given every kind of medal to be found in Russia! In the end, this mixture of different types doesn't shock me. It doesn't bother me that the two-headed eagle is the symbol of Tsarism. I'm also very fond of the hammer and sickle. They represented the union of worker and peasant, and that idea was a good one. In fact, I'd even have preferred Russia to keep that symbol. When people start to destroy, they overthrow everything that existed beforehand, even the good things. The hammer and sickle wouldn't look so bad on modern decorations.

When I received this decoration, war veterans sent me letters in which they waxed indignant that I'd accepted this medal, and called Yeltsin a traitor to the motherland. Some of them advised me to send it back to him. Personally, I take a different view. It was neither Yeltsin nor any other leader who awarded these decorations to me. It was the motherland herself, via her successive leaders, who was rewarding me.

In any case, Yeltsin decorated me several times: among other awards, he presented me with a weapon of honour. In former times, this was considered to be superior to a simple medal. These weapons are generally made of precious metals and engraved with the names of those for whom they are meant. So on this particular occasion I went to a reception given by Yeltsin at the Kremlin. He told me, 'You have obtained all the medals our country can give. So I am presenting you with this' And he opened a box. I glanced at it without really examining its contents. I thanked him, embraced him, gave my speech and went back to my hotel. As soon as I was back, I opened the box and found a perfectly ordinary, used pistol. I was hugely disappointed! I couldn't get over the fact they had presented me with such a thing. I returned to Izhevsk, filled with anger. All my friends were of the same opinion. So I dashed off a letter to Yeltsin. I corrected this letter at least ten times. It was rather vehement in tone. In it, I wrote that this mediocre decoration humiliated the President of Russia even more than it did me.

No sooner had my letter arrived than the telephone started to ring non-stop. It was Yeltsin's assistants. They asked me: 'But what's missing on that weapon of yours? Gold plating? We'll gold plate the pistol for you.' I refused, and retorted that the pistol had been presented to me in that state and that it would stay like that. I added that it was a perfectly commonplace pistol, which had already been used. And that I wouldn't mind at all if everyone got to know of the contents of this letter!

And in fact, when my museum opens, I'll put this pistol on exhibition together with my letter to the president. So that people can judge for themselves . . .

6

'AT HOME AND ABROAD'

Passing from the Soviet regime to untrammelled capitalism was a difficult trial for the majority of Russians, including Kalashnikov.

As soon as the USSR came to an end, at the start of 1992, the new regime under Yeltsin's leadership, drawing its inspiration from Western methods of 'shock therapy', took radical measures to reform the country's economy. A 35-year-old minister, Yegor Gaidar, freed prices, deregulated commerce and privatized state firms to create a middle class of entrepreneurs.

The result was a drastic lowering in the Russians' standard of living. In one year, prices shot up by more than 100 per cent. Uncontrolled capital accumulated. Privatization was catastrophic.

In 1992, Yeltsin launched 'vouchers', a kind of cheque that opened the way for people to have a small amount of private property. Shared out uniformly among the population, the vouchers were worth 10,000 roubles each, but they had to be

*invested in some enterprise. A year and a half later, inflation
had wrought havoc: the voucher was worth no more than three
or four bottles of vodka. Money placed in savings banks also
melted away even as people looked on: a great proportion of
the population was ruined.*

*The new Prime Minister, Viktor Chernomyrdin, authorized the
free buying and selling of shares. These were snapped up by the
bosses of different businesses. Then the government tried to
attract foreign investments, and auctioned off the biggest
businesses in the country. Thus it is that 80 per cent of production today is in the hands of private enterprise.*

*And the misfortunes of the new capitalist Russia contin-
ued: in 1998, following a fall in the price of petrol, a huge
financial crisis broke out – reserves of currency evaporated,
the miners who had not been paid rose in revolt, debt
repayments were suspended and the value of the rouble collapsed. Within one year, the average income of Russians fell
by 25 per cent. The country's economy was thoroughly
'dollarized'.*

*Later on, after several years of austerity, inflation was
brought under control. Industrial production and agriculture
slowly started to improve.*

IZHEVSK

I've been living in Izhevsk for 50 years, and I've had time to
develop quite a liking for this city.

Izhevsk was founded in 1760. It was a little market town;
it was destroyed in 1774 during Pugachev's famous rebellion
against Catherine II. The town was reborn in 1807 with the
building of a weapons factory, at the head of which was an
engineer of considerable talent: Deryabin.

It was only from 1867 that workers were allowed to work
there freely. Their standard of living in Izhevsk was much

higher than that of other Russian workers. The Izhevsk workers refused to accept the October Revolution. The Civil War and the Stalinist repressions did not spare the population – neither the clergy and the intelligentsia, nor the ordinary workers. At the start of the 1930s, almost all the churches were destroyed. There was in particular a very beautiful cathedral decorated with a Foucault pendulum. There were only two such pendulums in the whole of Russia – in Saint Petersburg and in our city. The cathedral was razed to the ground to make room for a school – which was never built. It was an incredible act of barbarity!

In 1934, the city became the capital of the autonomous republic of Udmurtia. It was a workers' town of the kind typically found in the Urals, with a factory in the middle and, adjoining the factory, a pond. Nearly half the inhabitants of Udmurtia lived in Izhevsk.

With the coming of the Soviet Union, the factory widened its range of productions, adding motorbikes, machine tools, on-board weapons for aviation, Simonov automatic rifles, Tokarev rifles and Kalashnikov assault rifles, and even components for space rockets.

During the war, the factory produced 12 million firearms – twice as many as were produced from all the factories in Great Britain!

* * *

At the start of 1948, I was ordered to take up an assignment in the Urals, in a factory in Izhevsk, where manufacture of my AK-47 was due to start. I imagined at the time that my stay in this city wouldn't last very long, and that afterwards I'd return to work at the Shurovo Polygon again. Katya and I had agreed that my family would continue to live there and wait for my return.

My wife's mother lived in the small town of Shurovo, just next to the Polygon, from which we derived great joy and satisfaction – after all, the grandmother is the essential element of the Russian family, the person you can count on in all circumstances. At least, this is how it was during my youth (and my wife has now become an exemplary babushka herself, but this happened long afterwards). Every day, the grandmother effectively bore the burden of a young couple's household worries. Our work didn't leave us with any time to take care of those things.

When I met my wife, she already had a little daughter, a one-year old, called Nellia. Katya's first partner worked with us at the Polygon.

It was only after we'd moved to Izhevsk that we got married. In those days, nobody bothered about the formalities of marriage. Nobody was shocked by people living together, or even having children outside marriage. At the end of September 1948, my wife gave me our first daughter, Elena. The clinic in which my wife gave birth was just downstairs from my mother-in-law's apartment. Every minute we kept going down to get the latest news. It was only on the morning of the second day that we were told of the birth of Aliona (this is the diminutive she was given when she was small). She resembled a Gypsy girl, with curly black hair. I myself had very thick brown hair at the time, but it wasn't curly. A few days after her birth, the little girl's hair also grew straight, to my great satisfaction.

In autumn 1949, after the definitive adoption of the AK-47 by the Soviet Army, I was demobilized and we all set off for Izhevsk, where I was to continue developing my weapon in the machines construction factory in that city.

My civilian life began. We initially stayed in the only hotel in Izhevsk, where, during the freezing cold nights, you could hear mice and rats scampering about. On one occasion, they almost ate Aliona: they had doubtless decided her bed would make a nice warm den. Katya only just rescued her. After this incident, we decided to all sleep together.

* * *

In the spring of 1950, we moved into a room in a shared apartment, and it was a great joy for us, even if it measured only twelve square metres. This apartment had three rooms in all, the two others being occupied by another family. We shared the same bathroom, toilets and kitchen, where the stove served for both families. (In those days, most of the inhabitants of Izhevsk lived in this type of apartment.)

We were lucky, since our neighbours were very nice people, hardworking and quiet. We made friends with them, and invited them round on holidays. They had a grown-up daughter who helped Katya look after the children. So this life of enforced proximity had its advantages! Nellia, who until then had been living with her grandmother, came to join us too.

Two years later, the factory allocated a two-roomed apartment just for us. This was a windfall. In 1953 my younger daughter Natasha was born. I'd been hoping for a boy, but I immediately fell in love with this fragile child. So there were five of us before Viktor arrived.

Before I met Katya, I'd had a son, Viktor, born in 1942 and baptized with this name in honour of my brother (this was in Kazakhstan, in the little town of Matai.) He still lived there with his mother. Viktor was only 15 when, in 1957, his mother perished in tragic circumstances, run over by a train. With my wife's agreement, we decided to adopt him.

I have to say that, before my marriage, I fell in and out of love as I moved from one place to another. Without being a Don Juan – I was in fact rather shy – I liked pretty girls. But my very poor visual memory left me with one great anxiety: I hoped I'd be able to recognize her the next morning!

I must confess that I've never had time to take a real interest in my children and family life. It was my wife who looked after all that, and she still had energy left over to be a very active representative of the pupils' parents at school. She was also the chair of the tenants in our block of flats, which was, at the time, an important task. I wouldn't usually get home from the factory before ten in the evening. Everyone in the family knew that my work was sacred. When the children misbehaved, my wife would put them in the corner, telling them they'd have to wait there until I got home. This was the most horrible punishment, since nobody knew when I would return.

After Stalin's death, my mother was finally able to come and visit. I hadn't seen her since the period of my escape from exile in Siberia! Katya was amazed to see that my mother, after so many years as a deportee, and despite having brought 18 children into the world, had stayed so youthful in appearance and character. What amused her a great deal, and delighted the children, was to see her drinking her tea while munching salted gherkins (molossols). Perhaps this was a memory from the faraway Caucasus where she had once lived, and where she'd been in the habit of munching salted watermelons: when she was deported, the gherkins had replaced the watermelons. During her stay, we spent many nights talking over our memories, and discussing all those years when we had practically been without any news of one another. I waxed ironic: 'Mother, can you believe that the little peasant boy I used to be has received the Stalin Prize?' And she invariably replied: 'Of course, Misha. I always knew you'd turn out to be someone important!'

I'm sure she was the one who transmitted a passion for molossols to me. The only domestic task I had to fulfil was preparing the marinades. Gherkins and salted cabbage were my speciality. My recipe consisted in putting the gherkins in a cask, lined upright like little soldiers, and covering them with a variety of leaves: oak, cherry, mulberry. I added horseradish and a few apples. Produce like this wasn't always available in the shops, being rather dear for a big family like ours and not as good as mine. As for fresh fruit and vegetables, they were an exorbitant price.

At the beginning of autumn, the whole family got into our brand-new Pobyeda with baskets and string bags, and we made our way to the big vegetable garden that was owned by our factory. It was here that we bought our fresh vegetables, picked directly from the field. They were much less expensive and of better quality than those from the shops. With our booty, we would make preserves that lasted all winter.

I've practically never taken a real holiday, and nor has my wife. We didn't go to the 'sanatoriums', as rest houses were called, and we didn't take part in any tourist excursions. The children, on the other hand, spent every summer at holiday camps for young pioneers, at which Lena, who was and has remained very sporty, won all the prizes.

In 1960, our living conditions improved considerably. The factory presented us with a cottage, of the 'Finnish house' type. These dwellings were given this name because they'd apparently been built after the war by Finnish prisoners. They were usually reserved for our factory managers. In fact, it was a real izba, modest in size but with four bedrooms, a veranda and even a cellar for those marinades of ours. There was also a tiny garden with fruit trees and a little vegetable garden, which I started to tend assiduously. Finally, we were able to afford the pets the children had long dreamed of: a dog, a cat, a tortoise and a squirrel. The dog, named Laddy, was my favourite. I used to take him with me on my infrequent hunting and fishing excursions, but since I spoiled him, he rapidly became something of a stay-at-home; at all events, he was never properly trained, and the other hunters reproached me for this. Trained or not, I doted on him. All my friends asked me what he was getting up to, and I told them the dog would soon be able to lift the telephone himself, since I was teaching him to speak.

Unfortunately, we were forced to move out once again, since they were apparently going to demolish our house to build a school. Twenty-five years later, the izba I loved so much is still there, and I always gaze at it nostalgically. But it has to be said that the new apartment we were allocated was very acceptable; in fact, I still live there. A four-bedroom apartment was considered a great luxury.

*　*　*

The children grew up and started to have children of their own. At 47, I became a grandfather for the first time: in 1966, Nellia had a daughter, and Viktor a son. Lena was studying at the Institute of Mechanics in Izhevsk, Viktor and Nellia were studying engineering. In 1972, Lena got married and had a son, Igor, whom I brought up as if he were my own son. Only Natasha, the littlest, stayed to live with us. She was addicted to her passion, dancing, which she did at a specialist school, but her precarious health meant she was obliged to abandon this discipline and study mechanics in Izhevsk.

My wife fell seriously ill when she was barely 50. The doctors diagnosed an infectious polyarthritis. They told her she would have to choose between a long life of illness, being frequently laid up in bed and eventually sentenced to immobility, or a few years of active life with the help of drugs that would have deleterious side-effects. She preferred the second option. From then on she underwent frequent bouts of treatment at the sanatorium and in the Kremlin clinic, to which I was entitled. She died at 51, after undergoing hormonal treatment, and I was left alone with Natasha.

Natasha was the most affectionate and the sweetest of all our children. She was the centre of gravity of our small group of friends. Relations between Igor, Elena's son, and Natasha, his aunt, were particularly close: he loved her like his own mother.

One day, Natasha had to travel to Moscow by train. For three days, the weather was so bad that no plane was allowed to take off. At the third attempt, Igor, who was 11, wanted to accompany her to the airport. I watched them through the window as they got into a taxi, and my heart was filled with a sense of foreboding that I was seeing Natasha for the last time. A few hours later, I was relieved when she phoned me from the airport: the planes were still unable to take off, and she was coming back home.

On the way home, she was sitting next to the taxi driver, who in fact was one of her old classmates. Igor was behind her. At a bend in the road, the driver lost control of his car and ended up in the wrong lane. There was a coach coming towards them; it ploughed into the car on the side where my daughter was sitting. She didn't die immediately. They pulled her out of the taxi and the first car that came along took her to hospital.

I didn't know any of this and was waiting patiently at home for them. Igor came back alone. I could immediately see the boy was in a state of shock. He told me, in a scarcely audible voice: 'We've had an accident. Natasha's been rushed to hospital'.

I phoned round every hospital in Izhevsk. She wasn't in any of them. In the end, I went to see the police. When they told me in a matter-of-fact way that my daughter was in the morgue, I refused to accept it. It was impossible – they must be mistaken. When I saw my daughter's body on a table of zinc, I almost lost my mind. I couldn't understand it at all: what was she doing there? I begged her to come back home.

That was 13 November 1983. We buried her next to her mother. She would have been 30 a few years later. After the death of these people I loved so much, I felt very lonely.

* * *

Ever since, I've led a solitary life, although my grandson Igor often comes to have dinner and sleep over at my house. After Natasha's death, he felt so unhappy he would even come and join me in bed. Now Igor is 30 and pursuing a commercial career. Nellia is a grandmother and her daughter got married in Columbia, so my great-grandson is Columbian.

Viktor has followed in my footsteps: he has become a weapons designer too, but *he* has earned all the diplomas you need! He works at the same factory as myself, and recently contributed to developing a prototype for one of my competitors. When he was a schoolboy, he was unaware of my profession. He was very keen on studying mechanics, so he went to the Izhevsk mechanics institute where he specialized in firearms; at this point he realized who I really was. At the end of his studies, he wrote a brilliant thesis on this special topic. Viktor took part in developing the prototype AK-47, and then the prototype of a hunting rifle. At the beginning of perestroika, his team started to manufacture special weapons for the Ministry of the Interior, including the Bison sub-machine gun, which is widely used by the militia in every Russian town.

Lena works in telecommunications in Izhevsk. In autumn 2002, she became president of the Kalashnikov Foundation (of which I am honorary president). She is the person who looks after my 'international' life and tries to defend my image against all attempts at fraud: no small task.

* * *

I have quite a good standard of living. Compared to the nouveaux riches Russians I'm a real pauper, but compared to ordinary Russians I'm well-off. For several years I've been living in my big four-room apartment, with nice furniture, filled with presents and souvenirs (from all of our successive heads of state) – but most of them have been set apart for the future Kalashnikov museum. A whole room, which I rarely let people into, is reserved for my decorations!

I've got a new dacha with a big garden. All my savings went into it. I'm very proud of this small, two-storey wooden house, the colour of honey. There are rooms for all the children, one for me and even an office, decorated with all my hunting trophies. This is the place where I prefer to work these days: I can see the lake from my window and, right up close, the trees I planted myself. I look after its upkeep by myself; together with DIY, it's become my favourite pastime. I use a lawnmower of my own invention, and my latest device is a trap to catch the moles that ruin my garden.

For my birthday, my son had given me a mole trap that cost a fortune and wasn't very easy to use. I told myself it was unbelievable that the Russians import mole traps from Germany! So I invented mine, which is much more efficient. People even suggested I should patent it. But can you imagine a 'Kalashnikov mole trap'? I refused, and it's still the only example of its kind.

I have three cars that my children use: a Ford, a Niva and a 4 × 4 for hunting. A driver comes to fetch me every morning and take me to the factory. Every day, I have lunch in the canteen of the Council of Ministers of the Republic of Udmurtia. There are many people worse off than me!

BETTER LATE THAN NEVER

The very first time I went abroad was to Bulgaria, at the start of the 1970s. My wife and I had holidayed in a famous seaside resort, the Golden Sands. In those days, it had become common for Soviet citizens to travel in socialist bloc countries. All the same, before I left, I'd been asked to go to the local KGB office.

The conversation was long and intense. I wish I'd recorded it: I'm sure it would have made an interesting article.

I received some instructions: our tourist group was to visit the city of Kazanlik, where the factory producing Kalashnikovs was situated. The Bulgarians were absolutely not to know who I was! In fact, not even the people in our group should know. The KGB made me choose an assumed name: Ivanov, Petrov or Sidorov. I think that certain people in the group had doubts about my identity, which always remained a 'military secret'. This made me feel very uneasy. When we reached Kazanlik, I was longing to take a tour round this factory! Unfortunately, this was quite impossible.

We went to the famous Shipka site,[1] where Russian soldiers, under the leadership of Generals Skobolev, Gurko and Dragomirov, fought at the sides of their Bulgarian brothers to free their country from the Turkish yoke. There is the most extraordinarily beautiful monument there. Before going to Bulgaria, I had read up on the Russian-Turkish war of 1877–8, and actually being there was a great moment for me.

I had another two opportunities to return there: in 1993 and 1995. These were business trips, undertaken at the invitation of the arsenal factory, where they produced replicas of my designs for assault rifles and machine guns.

We got on extremely well with the Bulgarian workers and engineers. I felt just as if I was in my own Izhmash factory! I even bumped into an old acquaintance, N. I. Korovyakov, a designer from the city of Tula, who now lives in Sofia. In Tula, he didn't have a very senior position, and his work wasn't properly appreciated, while in Bulgaria he was given the title of academician! I also had an opportunity to see Shipka again: this time, everyone knew who I was. And the Bulgarian Prime Minister made a point of meeting me there, and invited me to dinner.

* * *

Kalashnikovs are produced in China, in Romania and in several other countries. This is a gift from our country: all Warsaw Pact member states could manufacture Kalashnikovs in their own countries, without having to pay for the privilege. Initially, China started off reproducing the Russian model exactly, but subsequently the Chinese modified several components, such as the butt and the visor, though they didn't alter the essential design.

In 1991, I received a letter of invitation from a Chinese industrial group, asking me to visit their firearms manufacturing companies. The journey took place between 19 August and 2 September 1991, immediately after the putsch against Gorbachev. Here I was able to visit a Kalashnikov factory. I noticed that the workers did a great deal of the work by hand. The factory boss explained why they did it this way: it was so as to occupy the maximum number of workers! Apparently, the ones I saw worked only four hours a day, but the results were very good, just as good as in the other countries where production was mechanized.

They were set up in the same way as ours in the 1950s. But in other towns, I saw modern, well-lit factories. Their production was really rather good. The Chinese are a very hardworking people. I took advantage of the opportunity to visit several monuments, such as the Forest of Stones and the

Great Wall. I was deeply impressed: I'd never imagined I'd ever have such an opportunity.

During my visit to one production unit, there was a regrettable incident which had repercussions on the whole of my future life. I was firing with a small-calibre assault rifle with a sawn-off barrel. There was a helmet protecting my ears. A Chinese television team was filming us: a cameraman must have found I didn't look very handsome with my earflaps, and he suggested I take them off to look more photogenic. I was wrong not to protest, since the result was disastrous. The weapon with which I was firing was particularly noisy. After that session, my ears were buzzing and conversations came to me as if through cotton wool. I realized that my mistake was going to cost me dear. Ever since then, I've had difficulty hearing.

America was the first country in the capitalist bloc that I managed to visit.

My relations with the United States started quite a while ago, and came about in rather a strange fashion. In 1972, to my great surprise, I found in my letterbox a postcard from the United States. My position meant that I was obliged to report this straightaway to the KGB. So I went to see the head of the local KGB, an old acquaintance of mine. He was suspicious. 'So they're asking you for your life-story and a photo, are they?' he said. 'That's probably just for starters. What will they want from you after that? The prototypes of your weapon, no doubt? Ah – they want to write a book about you? Well, I suggest you consult the Party committee and get advice from them.'

But the regional boss decided to send me back to the KGB office! I told him that's where I'd just come from. So he suggested that I wait a while before replying. Nobody wanted to compromise themselves. A year later, I was phoned by the Foreign Ministry and asked whether I'd received a letter from an American historian who specialized in the history of weapons named Edward Ezell. At the Ministry, they were astonished that I hadn't replied! What a wonderful thing bureaucracy is.

It wasn't until 17 years after Ezell's first letter that I met him, in July 1989, in Moscow. Edward C. Ezell was the head of the historical service of the American Army, and the custodian of the collection of firearms in the National Museum of American History, attached to the Smithsonian Institute. He had come along with a film team, and I was interviewed over a period of several days.

The following year, I was to travel to the United States to continue to make a scientific documentary focusing on modern firearms designers, for the Smithsonian Institution. I struck up a close friendship with Ezell. We were like two youngsters who shared the same passion. The things he wrote about weapons in general, even about Russian weapons, are much more exhaustive and interesting than what the Soviets themselves have written on this subject. Unfortunately, Ezell died a few years after our meeting. I have carefully preserved his precious correspondence. In one of his letters, he wrote to me: 'As a firearms historian, I consider, without exaggeration or flattery, that you had a major influence on the development of that technology during the second half of the twentieth century. Everyone seems to agree on that. You played an important part in forming the contemporary world. This makes the process by which you created your designs of particular interest.'

You could say that Edward Ezell became my Christopher Columbus, since it was thanks to him that I discovered America! It's a shame this happened so belatedly. In my youth, I was fascinated by the tales of people who'd been off travelling, and I imagined myself in their place.

In 1990, when I received Ezell's invitation to go to the United States, it was pretty much the same as if I'd been invited to the Moon. I doubted whether such an adventure would be possible. Would I be allowed to leave the USSR? And if so, would I be allowed to enter American territory? We'd had it drummed into us that America was our number one enemy.

My daughter Elena and an interpreter accompanied me to the United States embassy in Moscow. I just had to obtain the visas. I had no idea what a difficult and tedious procedure this would be. If I had known, I'd have given up the idea straightaway! We arrived at the embassy very early in the morning, after spending a night in the train. There was whole crowd of people thronging the doors. Just to pick up the right forms we had to wait a whole three hours. And then the same length of time all over again to hand them in at the window. Finally, a young employee of the embassy attached some little stickers to our passports, and informed us that there wouldn't be any problem. But our interpreter had the bright idea of announcing to the employee that I was 'the' Kalashnikov, the one who had designed the AK-47. The young man's expression suddenly changed, and he tore our passports out of our hands, declaring that I'd need special permission from the American State Department, which would take another ten days!

Thanks to Ezell and my friendship with him, I was able to meet some famous weapons designers: Eugene Stoner[2] and Bill Ruger[3], who had built several American rifles and pistols, and Uzi Gal,[4] the inventor of the celebrated Israeli submachine gun, the 'Uzi'.

Stoner and I had taken part in the documentary film about modern weapons designers that was made for the archives of the Smithsonian Institution, which collects, preserves and exhibits the cultural, scientific and technical manifestations of our civilization.

I spent several days with Eugene Stoner, the designer of the M-16. There was considerable mutual respect between us. One day, a shooting session was organized in a field. I shot with his M-16 and he used a Kalashnikov AKM. 'The Kalashnikov has a different firing rhythm and sound', remarked a general who was present. And he added: 'During my career, I've had an opportunity on several occasions to hold Kalashnikovs taken from the enemy, and I could even have used them in the course of military operations. But because they sound different, I was afraid my own soldiers might take me for an enemy and start firing at me!'

In the United States, they say that Stoner was a mysterious figure. He didn't like the press and he practically led the life of a recluse. He started out as a mere industrial draughtsman. His first experience with weapons came during the war, when he worked initially on ammunition and then on automatic weapons. His M-16 was given its final shape only during the Vietnam War.

Stoner and I had many things in common. The struggle against fascism became, for both of us, a strong motivation to design a new weapon. Stoner was, just like me, self-taught. He'd not had any higher or specialist education. During the Second World War, he was a corporal in the Marines.

The Americans showed a special interest in me. Edward Ezell explained it in these terms: 'In the West, people are curious to find out about the major players in the Soviet military industry. By telling Kalashnikov's life story, we can understand how the Soviet army became independent of foreign designers by creating its own technology. We can also learn a little more about the man who has become a hero in his own country.'

Ezell added that the biggest weapons designers in the world, such as Stoner, considered my models to be the best there were. 'Certain specialists think that the M-16 has the same merits. Personally, I completely disagree. In the TV news, it's the AK-47 that you see in Beirut, in the Iranian desert, in the jungles of El Salvador, in the mountains of Afghanistan. In fact, this is what has impelled us Americans to take an interest in the personality of Mikhail Kalashnikov.'

Stoner was simple man, quite without arrogance or foolish self-satisfaction: quite the opposite – he treated me as a friend right from the start. He always pushed me forward at important meetings. He was three years younger than me. We'd been born in the same month, in November, under the same sign of the zodiac, and we even looked like one another, though he was taller. We wore similar clothes – a pullover and a light parka.

I noticed that Americans weren't too keen on inviting me into their homes. It seems to be a typically Russian habit to invite new acquaintances to your home straightaway.

There was one thing that made me very different from Stoner. I'd been decorated by my country with every possible award, every imaginable medal. At official meetings, I wore on my jacket my two stars for being a Hero of Socialist Labour and the gold badge of a Lenin Prize Winner, which Stoner gazed at with considerable interest. He had never received a single decoration from his government. On the other hand, he was extremely wealthy, and possessed his own plane and helicopter, and earned a certain sum of money for each of his M-16 assault rifles sold throughout the world.

I consider him as a very talented weapons designer. He died in 1997, after a long illness, asking the doctors to pull the plug on the machines that were keeping him alive.

In 1992, I returned to the United States at the invitation of Bill Ruger. I discovered the West Coast, the America of Cowboys and Indians. Ruger owned three factories. I visited one of them, in which I was apparently given a Hollywood film star's welcome. In 1993, I again met Uzi Gal. I saw him again in 1998, and this time we struck up a friendship. He died in September 2002 in the United States, but he was buried in Israel. Ruger too died recently. So I am the last surviving modern firearms designer!

Since my first tour of America, I have travelled almost 40 times outside Russian borders: to the United States, France, Germany, England, Switzerland, China, India, Columbia, Argentina, South Africa, Saudi Arabia, the United Arab Emirates, Jordan and many other countries.

In 1995, I was appointed consultant of the general director of the state firm Rosvoorujenie. When this was reorganized, I became a consultant for Rosoboronexport. As a delegate of this company, I took part in weapons fairs and conferences in several countries. The most recent took place in Jordan. It was devoted to the problems of the struggle against terrorism, the seizure of hostages and smuggling. The young King of Jordan, Abdullah II, came in person to give me a warm and respectful welcome.

But of all the countries I've visited, the one I like most is little Switzerland. Everything is so clean and shining there, even the cows!

Every time I come back home, my heart bleeds for my country, which is poor even though it has so many natural and human riches. I keep telling myself that Russia is a vast country that you can't compare with others, that it has suffered from so many cataclysms, and that the Germans ravaged half of it. Since then, 60 years have gone by and, frankly, we could have done better!

These days I receive huge numbers of invitations from the entire world, but I rarely accept them: after all, I am 83. On my birthday I receive telephone calls from the United States, Germany, France. Letters and faxes from these countries reach me without any problem. We've quickly forgotten the suspicious attitudes that were prevalent among us just 10 or so years ago. This is the positive side of perestroika, which opened us up to the outside world.

* * *

I've now worked for nearly 50 years at the Izhmash factory. This is a famous company that has specialized in weapons for two centuries. It was founded by a remarkable engineer: Deryabin. After privatization in 1991, Izhmash became a public company, and its decline began. This is no exception: many of the factories that worked for Defence collapsed at the same time. Quality specialists, both engineers and workers, lost their jobs and haven't found new ones.

Like many other people who worked at Izhmash, I received a certain number of shares that have brought me neither a dividend nor any power. I haven't become one of the 'owners' in the business that has for half a century been producing weapons that bear my name. The privatization of our factory hasn't made a capitalist of me!

The transferral of property from the state to the private sector is no cause for rejoicing as far as I am concerned. Not that I'm opposed to people being better-off, but I can't accept that the wealth produced by several generations of Russians should all pour, in record time, into the pockets of certain individuals. I'm sure this won't bring prosperity to our country. The nouveaux riches Russians are now notorious throughout the entire world!

It's true that I'm a pure product of the socialist system: you may say that I'm 'the last of the dinosaurs'. Too bad. All my life I considered I was working for my country and not in order to build up my own property. Everything I have done in my life belongs to Russia.

Despite this, people have sometimes tried to lure me into 'capitalist ventures'. With my socialist ideas, especially when they come with a total lack of understanding of the juridical system, it was a real catastrophe.

In 1992, I was informed that the decision to set up a public company called 'Kalashnikov' had been taken at government level. I must admit that, to begin with, this filled me with a certain pride. The 'Kalashnikov firm' created an impression of reliability and authenticity! The arguments put forward to convince me to give my name to this enterprise were still thoroughly socialist ones: it was necessary for the good of our country, our factory, and the people who were jobless and without resources.

The plan was for the 'Kalashnikov public company' to combine all the firms in our republic of Udmurtia, and I gave my agreement without discussing the conditions of my appointment as honorary president. I naively thought that I'd be able to keep control over the way my name was used. I was greatly disappointed when I realized that I had no rights within 'my' company! I would like to have had at least the possibility of withdrawing my name if its image didn't correspond with what I wanted from it. It transpired that this wasn't written into the statutes.

As it happens, this company has never exported weapons or any other military equipment, and I am really delighted that no sale of weapons has been carried out in my name.

In 1996, Izhmash started to produce Saiga hunting rifles based on the modernized AK, and the factory set up a semi-public company with the Americans, giving it my name, Kalashnikov. Yet again, I was persuaded to accept it for the good of our factory and our workers. I think the company is indeed running, but I haven't heard a whisper of its activities, and I don't derive any profits from it. I haven't even signed a contract with this company.

I want everyone to know, once and for all, that I have no connection with any foreign company that produces and sells Kalashnikov weapons abroad!

These days, I have at my disposal a foundation aimed at protecting my image and my name from any kind of fraud.

ODDS AND ENDS

I've dedicated my whole life to designing and improving the AK. If a thing's worth doing, it's worth doing well. A dilettante never does anything properly. Parodying the poem by Pushkin, I wrote one day: 'I have erected a monument to myself thanks to my own relentless work, and the soldiers will always beat a path to visit it.[1] Yes, I really and truly believe that soldiers will be forever grateful to me!

At the age of 83, I continue to work, from 8 in the morning to 5 in the evening. I get up very early every morning: I'm already up at 5 a.m. Still, I do rest three days a week; I always take Fridays off. At the moment, our work in the factory is essentially focused on designing hunting weapons.

I receive even more letters than in the past. Many people are simply asking me for my autograph. In the West, they're apparently mad keen to get it. I even wonder if certain people don't then sell it off! Too bad: I still send it to them. I receive a great number of Russian reviews, and foreign reviews that people translate for me.

Recently, I've become a bit like those generals in Chekhov who got invited to every wedding. I am obliged to be there at every festivity, great and small, in the Republic of Udmurtia. And most of the time, the speeches are followed by receptions. There are far too many celebrations and anniversaries for my taste. People have started commemorating everything and anything: every little event has its first anniversary, its second, its tenth – it's the flavour of the month: a never-ending festivity. The creative spirit is flagging, but not when it comes to receptions.

So I've become a celebrity, but I haven't got big-headed about it. I'm getting old. My visual memory plays tricks on me, more than it used to. I don't recognize certain people I met in the past: so they think I'm snubbing them! To guard against this, I'd rather say hello to someone I don't know, but then they'd say the old bloke's gone completely gaga.

Still, some people seem to take umbrage at my celebrity. They sometimes say I prevent young talents from blooming. There are apparently prototypes that are twice as good as the Kalashnikov. When I hear this, I feel offended! It's annoying and completely wrong; as if I could ever stop anyone inventing anything.

Any technology can and should be improved. I think you always need to have a very precise and concrete aim in view if you're going to obtain good results. I don't think any inventor can now invent things that are completely and totally new. His inventions are obtained on the basis of pre-existing elements. A real inventor never stops doing research. The process of thinking never leaves him, wherever he may be.

Sometimes, when I devise a specific mechanism, it happens that I derive ideas from the equipment that people use in everyday life, and transfer these ideas to my plans. For example, while repairing a door bolt, I came up with an idea that I could use elsewhere. For the first of my inventions, I used pieces from alarm clocks. I lost count of the ones I ruined on this occasion! Ever since I was a child, and right up to now, I've dismantled and reassembled every possible kind of mechanism. I've broken quite a few of them, but I've also repaired several.

When the commissions judging my prototypes gave their opinions and pointed out the faults in my constructions, I was obliged to make corrections. For this, I had to think through the problem as a whole, not seeing the faults separately but as part of the whole, while always focusing on the essentials. And it often happened that I spent less time correcting a major fault than when I was correcting a trifling error, which could force me to modify the way the whole mechanism functioned.

When I set myself an object to be realized, I become very restless. I think about it night and day, until I achieve this objective. Perfection has no limits, does it?

These days, people have lost any interest in working and inventing. Everyone, or almost everyone, wants to get into business. In Izhevsk, for example, there isn't a single cellar or a single street corner which hasn't been transformed into a shop. Even the basements of houses are used as sales outlets. Nobody wants to put in any elbow grease any more, though the Russian people had always considered work as a point of honour.

I am proud of my life's work, and particularly of my invention when it is used for the liberation of peoples. But when it is used to oppress others, well of course, it breaks my heart. If my weapon is sometimes used for the wrong ends, I don't feel responsible: I've never had any power of decision, except over the plans of my own prototypes. I don't in any way feel responsible for the current situation in the world: I've never played any part in political life.

Was the path chosen after the 1917 Revolution the right one? Or did we lose our way? I would claim that the socialist ideas of the Revolution were the right ones. Obviously, a revolution entails chaos, and innocent victims. It's rather like a tornado: and the same was true of the French Revolution!

Lenin's ideals – equality between human beings, the rights they should enjoy – are still close to my heart. They were progressive ideas. When I speak of equality between human beings, I don't mean an absurd, uniform equality. Obviously, everyone can't all be the same. But as for granting the same rights to everyone, as a start – that's something I consider noble and just. I regret that Lenin died too prematurely, when Soviet power hadn't been properly formed. Perhaps he'd have given it a better shape. For me, Lenin was a genius.

When I was a boy, we were taught at school that Trotsky was an enemy of the people – so, naturally, we believed that he was. In spite of all the tragedies that were unfolding around us, we always trusted our leaders, our 'guides'! After Trotsky had been declared an 'enemy of the people', no one was ever prepared to remember his merits. And yet Trotsky was one of the founders of the Red Army. In spite of everything I've been able to read about him, I find it difficult to make up my mind. The articles on this topic are often subjective and sensationalist. We'll need more than a decade to study the documents dating from the revolutionary period, and the memoirs of its survivors, to lift the veil on the mysteries of the October Revolution. I think that history, like a good wine, needs time before it can be judged at its true value.

* * *

I was a Communist, and I still have my Party card. If I didn't believe in the success of Communism, I nonetheless believed in its ideals, and I was really sickened when I saw all those so-called Communists who, when Yeltsin came to power, were the first to grab the country's wealth.

The important thing isn't the name of the party in power, but its programme and, above all, its results. This name really has no importance whatsoever. These days I don't consider myself as belonging to any party. I'd like to be neutral and not get mixed up in politics. None of the existing parties meets with my approval. The Communists are not behaving properly. As for individuals such as Yavlinksy[2] or Zhirinovksy[3], I simply can't take them seriously. A few years ago, Luzhkov, the current mayor of Moscow, persuaded me to enter his party, 'Motherland'. I was a card-carrying member of this party, but it has since been dissolved. I'm not sure it's such a good thing to have a great number of different tendencies. The system I like best is where there are only two parties: the one can criticize the other.

We are living through a period in which everything is changing very fast. Who is still able to feel the wind that blows from the October Revolution? Zuganov[4] and his party aren't real Communists.

Gorbachev bears a great deal of the responsibility for the fate of the peoples of the ex-USSR. He was still in post as President when Yeltsin organized his plot at Belovezhskaya Pushcha.[5] And yet all he needed to do was send a commando unit to nip this plot in the bud. A president has to know what's going on behind his back; and Gorbachev didn't have enough of a firm hand. As a result, he endorsed the brutal collapse of the USSR and the creation of the CIS (what an infuriating name!)

The 1991 putsch[6] is particularly clear in my memory. The day before, I'd received my visa to travel to China. My son Viktor and I arrived in Moscow, and when we got to the hotel, we learned the news. We were supposed to be leaving the next morning, and the flight was still going ahead. No precise details about events were available. So we decided to leave. On our arrival, a Chinese interpreter told us, in Russian: 'All the conspirators have been arrested.' I was terribly anxious. The domestic peace of Russia was under threat. I've always been opposed to conflicts within the country. The law must in all cases be respected. Gorbachev again showed how weak he was in this episode. He didn't behave as the leader of a great country should have done, and I feel no pity for him. He isn't a strong-willed man.

As for Yeltsin, no, I really don't like him. The siege of the Russian Parliament was a scandal in the eyes of the whole world. We made ourselves look ridiculous. I wonder if he wasn't drunk when he gave the order to fire on the deputies of his own country, whatever their stance. How could a man in such a position of responsibility ever find it in his heart and his conscience to command tanks to fire on his own people? When I saw that, I went mad with rage. I picked up my pistol: I was ready to fight. Yeltsin's action was unjustifiable and unpardonable. He really deserved to be punished.

He was often shown on television in a state of (advanced) intoxication. This didn't inspire the Russian people with confidence. You started to wonder whether intelligent and competent people, able to behave in a decent fashion, could still be found in Russia. Yeltsin and Gorbachev, his predecessor, are the kind of people who easily sell out. When I was a deputy, I dealt with leaders of the Communist Party, who occupied very senior posts in the regions. I thought these were men of rock-hard principle, who would be shaken by nothing. Along comes Yeltsin, and gathers together a few of his cronies, and they all sign a ukase that destroys our great country. And all those big shots in the Party start scrabbling for the nation's riches! Up until now I can't see anything positive that's happened since the fall of the Soviet Union. Am I supposed to be pleased that some children get taken to school in a Mercedes, while others are reduced to rummaging around in dustbins? At least in the Soviet period you didn't see that.

As for foreign policy, we're no better off. We beat Germany and reached Berlin. And now we're having to beg from them. I find this rather nauseating. I think that what we should have done was force the Germans to pay for everything they destroyed in our country. They did such terrible damage that they owed us reparations, and instead we've been reduced to begging for aid from them.

On the other hand, there's the Berlin Wall! Was there really any need to build it? I don't know. When it comes to the Great Wall of China, that's understandable: they were trying to protect themselves from invaders. But to build a wall that divides the same people, that's something I *can't* understand. That wall cost us a great deal. Anyway, they knocked it down, so what was the point of building it? It reminds me of the labours of Sisyphus.

These days, Russia is more or less ready to enter NATO. It's our misfortune that we often have no real sense of logic. Russia is already surrounded by the armies of NATO. This won't lead to anything good, in my opinion. That the Ukraine wants to enter comes as no surprise to me, but that Russia should be making discreet appeals for membership saddens me. I just can't understand it: it flies in the face of all the ideas they inculcated us with. In fact, nobody knows what America's real plans for Russia are: you'd think that what would best suit the USA would be for Russia to break up.

And the economic situation is no better. I can see that the products of the land can be sold, but the land itself cannot. We extract petrol in unlimited qualities, and export it to the four corners of the world, but we don't spare any thought for those who will live after us. We don't reflect that all this wealth might one day be useful for them. If only the profits went to the state, I could understand, but everyone knows perfectly well that it only benefits a small number. Some grow rich, while others are sinking deeper and deeper into poverty. The privatization of land, a measure that is being prepared, will merely increase the gap. It won't be peasants who buy it. 'Land for the peasants' was one of the mottoes of the Revolution, and it has become an accepted tenet of our people. In the Altai, a single peasant can't accomplish anything. People there say that it's not land they're short of, it's petrol for the tractors, so they can sow and harvest. It's cooperative farms that they need. Russia is a huge country, and there's enough land for everyone. You'd think that it's only Moscow where they're short of land – to build dachas for the 'nouveaux riches' Russians!

Production is stagnating in our country, and the poverty that people live in is a terrible sight.

On the Izhevsk-Moscow line, the train stops at Vekovka station. In this small town there is a cut-glass factory. For a long time now, the factory has stopped paying its workers' wages. Instead, the workers just get cut-glass ornaments that come out of the factory. They then sell them on the platform. Every time a train comes by, they rush up to the doors and start trying to sell their merchandise to the passengers, even in the middle of the night. It's a surreal spectacle: the sellers jostle one another in the snow, and you can hear the sound of breaking glass. They call out to the passengers, vaunting their wares (which are indeed very pretty and of good quality), and letting them go for derisory prices. They lower their prices as time goes by, and before the train leaves, their cries turn into laments: 'Buy, sir, do buy! I'm letting you have it for next to nothing. I haven't been paid for a whole year, and I've got to feed my children'. Woe betide anyone who ventures onto the platform! He'll be literally swallowed up by the sellers.

I occasionally buy a few things at Vekovka station. I take advantage of this to talk to the workers and sellers. Recently, I bought a little vase from a woman, who wept as she told me that she was very happy that she could at last sell her merchandise, even if she had to come along in the middle of the night. A few years earlier it had been forbidden, and the militia would drive the sellers away with a hail of blows from their batons. I cannot begin to describe the state of sadness into which this story plunged me. How could such a thing happen to them, to me, to all of us? I had the impression that our dreams, like the cut-glass products of Vekovka, had been brutally trampled underfoot.

I have dedicated 50 years of my life to the factory at Izhmash, I have fought for it to become prosperous. And what has been the result? In my factory, too, wages are not being paid.

Personally speaking, of course, it would never occur to me to complain about my own situation. At the factory, I currently earn 15,000 roubles per month.[7] I also receive my pension as an ex-general. It is automatically paid into my savings account. I don't even know how much I've got, but it can't be a huge amount.

The result of all this poverty is alcoholism and drugs. Today, when I look out of my window at the secondary school opposite, I see young people taking drugs – it's pitiful!

I'm opposed to tobacco, especially in the case of women. However beautiful she may be, I take an instant dislike to a woman if she smokes. My son and my grandsons smoke. But in my apartment, I forbid the use of tobacco, even if I have a distinguished guest; I oblige him to go out into the stairwell.

Things used to be different. When you saw minors smoking a cigarette, you didn't hesitate to give them a clip around the ear, even if you weren't their parent. In addition, people drank much less. There's no comparison. Yes, people used to get drunk, but only at parties and on grand occasions. When I was young, people couldn't get alcohol as easily as they can today. As for drugs, they appeared on a massive scale after the collapse of our country.

These days, young men no longer have any desire to join the army. Their parents pay so that they can avoid military service. We were proud to belong to the Red Army. Personally, I was very happy when I was called up; I knew I would be able to study the technology that interested me.

Since the break-up of the USSR, people's mentality has changed, they've started to be afraid of each other. At the bottom of my apartment block they've installed a security door. What more can they do to protect themselves from delinquents?

In our prisons, there's a whole army of criminals awaiting execution. If it was up to me, I wouldn't hesitate to execute them – the murderers, that is, of course. What's the use of feeding them, letting them go on outings, turning them into media figures? There are even some who manage to escape and kill again. I'm not against the death penalty. I share Solzhenitsyn's opinion on this point even if, in other respects, I don't share his hatred of every aspect of Soviet life.

* * *

I probably owe the successes in my career to my perseverance. I've always worked hard ever since I was a small child. When I was young, I looked after the children who were younger than me – that was bloody hard work! My parents 'lent' me to the neighbours so I could help them out in the fields. I've never shrunk from physical labour. I can do everything, all the peasant's jobs – sowing, ploughing, milking the cows . . .

But more than anything else, what I like is order. In everything. Order, beauty and perfection: that's the school in

which I have forged my soul. And even now, at my age, if I
see a piece of paper that's been left lying around, I immediately pick it up. At home everything is very tidy, and I do the
housework myself. If this were not the case, I couldn't live or
work there.

In my dacha, if I catch sight of a fly, I declare a state of
emergency! I can't rest until I've crushed it.

I also like to do DIY in my apartment. In the 1950s, I'd
spotted an original kind of dresser for putting the washing-
up in. I made one for myself based on that model, then I
made some others which I gave as presents to my friends. I
tried to make them perfect, as with everything I do. I'm in
the habit of finishing everything I start: this is also one of my
main character traits.

I live alone, but I want everything around me to be nice to
look at. You'll never see dirty washing-up in my home. My
motto is: 'Everything should be neat and tidy and, in addition, should be a pleasure to look at.'

But nothing human is foreign to me. I love fishing, hunting and women. I think I'm a bon vivant. The happiest day
of my life was the day I emerged from my mother's womb!

Love has been always there in my life. I wasn't Don Juan,
but I've always been moved by the beauty of women. I think
a woman owes it to herself to be beautiful. I don't like to see
women doing hard manual work. It makes them lose their
femininity.

These days, it's reading that fills my life. I never had
much formal education. I always had so much work that I
was never able to attend a proper course. On the other
hand, I've learnt quite a lot from books. I especially like
'useful' books, those that can teach me something about
history, politics, technology. The minute my grandson
brings a new book along, I snatch it out of his hands so I
can read it first!

At the moment, I'm reading Seneca and Montesquieu. I'm in the habit of underlining all the passages I've dwelt on so I can mull over them. At the end of every book I finish, I sign the last page: this for me is the proof that I've read it right to the end.

I'm sometimes asked, by Western journalists in particular, whether I wouldn't rather live abroad. I generally reply by quoting a poet who is very close to my heart, Sergei Esenin:

> *'Leave Russia, come to paradise!'*
> *'I don't need paradise, I want to live in my*
>   *Motherland.*
> *'There isn't any paradise*
> *Outside my Russian land.'*

* * *

For a long time I have been haunted by the same recurrent nightmare: I'm walking at night along an unknown road, and I know I'll have to carry on walking for a good long while before I see the least flicker of light. I quicken my pace, then I break into a run. I have the curious presentiment that I mustn't give in to sleep, that there's some danger lying in wait for me. I'm overwhelmed by a dreadful sense of anguish: will I have the strength to reach my goal? This baleful dream still pursues me even these days.

There's something mystical in all that, but I'm not in the least a believer. When I was a boy, I was forced to say my prayers. My parents were religious people. I carried out the Orthodox rites as they asked me to, but I didn't believe in any of it. In those days, religion had already fallen into disgrace in the eyes of the authorities, and very few people dared to practise it.

All the same, I think religion can be useful. It enables you to find a moral framework. In the Russia of today, all ideals have been destroyed – so what's going to replace them? Personally, I believed in Lenin, in Stalin, in equality between men. I still think that nobody should have any right to oppress his neighbour, and that everyone should be given a fair chance. I like these lines from a poem by Lomonosov: 'Come, my friend, your feet are bare, your body is dirty, and your chest is hardly covered. Don't be ashamed, that doesn't matter: it's the start of the path of glory for many people.'[8]

*   *   *

A short while ago, the President of the Republic of Udmurtia offered to have a residence built for me, where I could have both my apartment and my museum. I declined his offer, for fear that hordes of visitors would end up skinning me alive. Anyway, it was too small for a museum dedicated to Kalashnikov weapons, which I hope one day to see with my own eyes. Right now, it's being built, slowly but surely. Construction began five years ago! Two storeys are vaguely starting to resemble something.

The Kalashnikov museum will include all the models of weapons that have been produced by our factory. They won't just be firearms and Kalashnikovs, but also models built by designers working at the factory these days, such as the talented weapons designer Nikonov. He has created an automatic weapon that in certain ways surpasses mine, but its mechanism seems very complicated: it lacks simplicity and reliability. In these respects, nobody has yet outstripped me. In terms of precision of aim, the Kalashnikov isn't the most high performing of modern assault rifles but, on the other hand, its simplicity means that the soldier can understand it easily. And for a soldier to love his weapon, he needs to understand it and know that it won't let him down. This has always been my aim. The Kalashnikov is the mother of a great family of weapons. I've spent my life working on it. And unfortunately, the world still needs it. I know perfectly well that firearms will be the last to disappear.

* * *

Recently, I also set up a Kalashnikov Foundation, and I'd like to dedicate myself to it so I can help young designers, not just in the domain of weapons, but in every domain. It could have a great future. I'd like to establish a system of prizes for the best. A lot of time has already been wasted: five or seven years ago, it would have been easier to pick up state subsidies and private donations. These days, there is a huge number of foundations of every kind, none of them much use. I'd be surprised if we manage to raise sufficient money. It would have been marvellous to be able to create a foundation like the Nobel foundation. I'd have done so straightaway, if I'd had any money. But holding your cap out to beg is something I don't feel capable of. I'd so like to be able to say: 'I may be on my way out, but I'm leaving a heritage to the best inventors of the future, those who will serve humanity.' But alas, I'm a king without a crown.

* * *

In 1998, I went to Volgograd (ex-Stalingrad) to celebrate the 55th anniversary of the Battle of Stalingrad: the battle, at least, hasn't changed its name. To begin with I went to visit the Mamayev hill. On it there rises a huge monument representing a woman brandishing a sword: this is the Motherland, whose sons and daughters defended the city. That day, many veterans gathered together, trying to meet up with old comrades from their regiment. They embraced each other, weeping, and remembering all those who perished here. I too was overwhelmed by memories.

In autumn 1941, the Germans were sweeping towards Moscow. They had even set a date for the city to be captured: 16 October. Our regiment was fighting in the Bryansk region. When I was wounded, that same month of October, battles were already raging close to Moscow. In the hospital, in the small town of Yelets, we, the wounded, refused to accept that the capital might fall. When it was announced that there would be a parade on Red Square on 7 November, we yelled with joy. If Stalin and the government were in Moscow, the capital would never surrender to the enemy. We were counting on the cold of winter, which has always been a friend of Russian soldiers. The battle for Moscow lasted until the end of April 1942: this was the Red Army's first victory and Hitler's first defeat since the start of the war.

On 6 December 1941 the first Red Army counteroffensive was launched. The hospital was bubbling over with excitement: everyone wanted to leave and go to the front. This was the time when I was starting to draw the first sketches of my sub-machine gun, naively hoping it would be put into production straightaway so as to defeat the enemy.

In 1942, when I was sent to the Polygon for the first trials on my weapons, the Battle of Stalingrad was just beginning. We followed events with trepidation. The capture of the city would have been a catastrophe: the front would have been split in two. Stalingrad stretched out for 50 kilometres along the Volga: we hoped it would form a barrier that the Germans would be unable to cross. They bombarded the city from morning to night: the artillery never fell silent. All those who could contribute to the defence were on the breach day and night. But soon the Germans broke through to the Volga, in the city centre. Fighting broke out in the streets. A million bombs were dropped in the course of the assault, and 500 tanks took part. The Germans were used to bringing entire countries to their knees in just a few weeks, but here they needed several months to cross a single street, several weeks to capture a house. And even when the enemy managed to take a house, they still had to fight for it storey by storey. In the Polygon, we too were on a war footing. Everyone sensed how close the front was. Sometimes the weapons designers would go up the front lines to try out their new weapons, and they did not always come back. On the walls of every office were pinned up big maps of the USSR. On them, every day, the changing shape of the fronts was indicated, and the routes our colleagues would need to take.

Work ended only when we heard the news bulletins from headquarters.

On 20 November 1942, Soviet troops finally took the initiative on the Stalingrad front. A hundred hours after the start of operations, the two fronts met up: that of Stalingrad and that of the south-west. All in all, 330,000 fascist soldiers were encircled in a pocket around the city. Fighting continued until the start of February 1943: on 8 January, High Command had sent an ultimatum to General von Paulus, and on 2 February his troops capitulated, with the loss of 147,000 men, while 90,000 of them were taken prisoner, including 24 generals. The Battle of Stalingrad had lasted five months!

Our joy was immense. If we were then convinced that the war would be over that same year, I still hoped that my sub-machine gun would see active service, since I knew that our soldiers were falling in combat with old sub-machine guns in their hands.

Gazing at the statue of the Motherland, with the sword in her hand, I thought, 'Little Mother, I came too late to present you with that sword. But the one that you carry today was forged by me!'

*   *   *

One day, when I was still a kid, my sister's husband, a committed Communist, asked me, 'What will you do when you grow up?' I told him I'd be an inventor. He refused to believe me, and pulled my leg: 'With *your* education?' But I was convinced that I'd manage to invent something. This certainty was deeply rooted in me. And I replied, 'I've already practically devised a perpetual motion machine!'

For my brother-in-law, of course, these were just boyish dreams. But much later, when the plans of my assault rifle were accepted, I took great pleasure in reminding him of our conversation!

The idea of creating something never left me. I began by putting bicycles together. I'd spend my time taking locks and padlocks apart and putting them together again, and sometimes I'd manage to repair them. In fact, I was unwittingly preparing myself for a 'career' as an inventor: a hard but thrilling life.

I have followed my path, rather as if I were being guided towards a precise goal. And I think I have followed the right road. If I'd stayed where we had been deported to, my life would have quite different. When I think over my life, I accuse nobody, but I forgive nothing. That's how it all happened. There you have it: it was destiny.

* * *

Today, I can weigh up my profits and losses.

I have been one of the pillars of our military-industrial complex, one of the most faithful servants of that military industry that has enabled Russia to keep its position on the international scene.

In all my life, I've never hurt anyone. My conscience is clear. I might have become someone else. But I became a weapons designer, and I don't regret this – I've never regretted it and I never will. I love Russia whatever happens, even if the messes it has repeatedly got into, in the past and the present, cause me pain.

History's bursts of gunfire have not spared my family. My father was still not 50 when he died in exile in Siberia, exhausted by hard labour. My brothers Ivan and Andrei perished in the war, as did Yegor, my sister Niura's husband. My brother Vasili returned from it an invalid. Nikolai, the youngest of the children, died prematurely: he was the one who was most affected by our childhood privations in Siberia. My brother Viktor was detained for seven years in the most fearful Gulag, that of the construction works on the Byelomorkanal.

People say that my life has been a success. I have devoted my existence to creating and perfecting the defence weaponry of the Soviet Union. This is the image that I would like to leave in history.

I have come full circle. I have received every honour and every medal. In my home village, from which we were once banished, my bust now rises in the middle of the main square!

NOTES

Preface

1 Pierre-Jean de Béranger (1780–1857) was a popular French poet and songwriter. [Tr.]

2 Étienne de la Boétie (1530–63) was a lawyer whose major work, the *Discourse on Voluntary Servitude*, was fiercely critical of tyranny. [Tr.]

Chapter 1 Treading a path of pain and sorrow

1 Altai: A Russian region close to Kazakhstan and Mongolia.

2 Nikolai Alekseyevich Nekrasov (1821–77): famous Russian poet.

3 Kulak: a 'rich' peasant in the Soviet sense – one who owned a big farm.

4 Bielomorkanal: a canal linking the White Sea and Lake Onega. This was a particularly gruelling construction site for the detainees forced to labour on it.

5 Tomsk: a city in western Siberia, near Novosibirsk.

6 Members of a religious community that had lived on the margins of the official Orthodox Church ever since the seventeenth-century schism.

Chapter 2 'Arise, great country! Arise to mortal fight!'

1 The beginning of the most famous Soviet song of the Second World War.

2 Fedor Vasilyevich Tokarev (1871–1968): Russian weapons designer.

3 Georgi Konstantinovich Zhukov (1896–1974): Marshal, principal Soviet military leader during the Second World War. He countersigned the German capitulation in May 1945. Stalin and later Khrushchev relied on him, but also took umbrage at his popularity.

4 Hugo Schmeisser: famous German weapons designer, inventor in particular of the first submachine gun, the MP-18, in 1918. He died in East Germany, in 1953.

5 Vasili Alekseyevich Degtyarev (1879–1949): Russian weapons designer.

6 Vladimir Grigoryevich Federov (1874–1966): Russian weapons designer, considered to be the father of Soviet automatic rifles.

7 Georgi Semyonovich Shpagin (1897–1952): Soviet weapons designer, inventor of the PPSh-41 sub-machine gun.

8 Nikolai Nikolayevich Voronov (1899–1968): he was in charge of Soviet artillery. He was appointed Marshal in 1944.

9 Yakov Ustinovich Roshchepei (1879–1958): an ordinary soldier in the army, who invented a rifle of a completely new design.

10 Anatoli Arkadievich Blagonravov (1894–1975): academician, and general in the Soviet artillery.

11 Sergei Gavrilovich Simonov (1894–1986): Russian weapons designer, who created in particular an automatic rifle, an anti-tank rifle and the celebrated semi-automatic rifle, the SKS-45.

Chapter 3 *The birth of the AK*

1 John Cantius Garand (1888–1974): Canadian designer. The American army adopted his celebrated M-1 rifle in 1936.

2 Aleksei Ivanovich Sudayev (1912–46): Soviet weapons designer, inventor of the PPS-43 sub-machine gun.

3 Izhevsk is the capital (population 700,000) of the Republic of Udmurtia, situated to the west of the Urals, between Kazan and Perm. Kalashnikov would later settle there definitively.

4 Edward C. Ezell (1939–93): world-famous historian and arms expert. He was the director of a department in the National Museum of American History, in the Smithsonian Institute, in Washington.

5 Izhmash: Russian abbreviation for 'Izhevsk machine construction factory'.

Chapter 4 *A unique weapon*

1 Dmitri Fyodorovich Ustinov (1908–84): Soviet Marshal, Minister in charge of armament during the war. On his death, the city of Izhevsk was renamed 'Ustinov', but the inhabitants decided, a few years later, to re-establish its former name.

Chapter 5 *'He was a god, he might rise again'*

1 Mikhail Vasilyevich Isakovsky (1900–73): Soviet poet. He wrote, among other things, the words of several songs that became very popular (for example, 'Katyushka').

2 Valentina Vladimirovna Tereshkova (born in 1937): in 1963 she became the first woman cosmonaut in the world. She went on to enjoy an important political career within the Party apparatus.

Chapter 6 'At home and abroad'

1 Shipka: a mountain pass where the Russian and Bulgarian forces repulsed the Turks, during the 1877–8 war.
2 Eugene M. Stoner (1922–97): designer of the famous M-16 American rifle and numerous other weapons (he registered almost a hundred designs during his lifetime).
3 William B. Ruger (1916–2002): founder of the biggest American firearms firm.
4 Uzi Gal (1923–2002): Israeli weapons designer.

Chapter 7 Odds and ends

1 A reference to Alexander Pushkin's poem 'Exegi Monumentum'. [Tr.]
2 Grigori Alekseyevich Yavlinsky: liberal economist, leader of the Yabloko party.
3 Vladimir Wolfovich Zhirinovksy: leader of the ultranationalist party the LDPR (the Liberal Democratic Party of Russia).
4 Gennadi Andreyevich Zuganov: leader of the KPFR (the Communist Party of the Russian Federation). This party, the successor of the Communist Party of the USSR, plays an important role in the Duma, the Russian Parliament, even though it doesn't enjoy a majority.
5 Belovezhskaya Pushcha: a locality near Brest in Byelorussia, where, on 8 December 1991, the presidents of Russia, the Ukraine and Byelorussia decided to dissolve the USSR and form the Community of Independent States (CIS). Mikhail Gorbachev resigned on 25 December.

6 In August 1991, an attempted *coup d'état* threatened the power of Mikhail Gorbachev, President of the USSR, for several days. This putsch marked the beginning of the disintegration of the USSR.

7 About 500 euros (2002 values).

8 Mikhail Vasilyevich Lomonosov (1711–65): world-famous Russian scientist and writer. He founded the University of Moscow.

GLOSSARY

Breechblock/breechblock apparatus
On the Kalashnikov, this is another term for the bolt carrier and rotating bolt. The bolt carrier is sometimes called the breechblock slide and the rotating block is sometimes called the breechblock. Inside the rotating block, running down its length, is a thin pin that fires the bullet when struck from behind by the hammer operated by the trigger.

Assault rifle
An assault rifle is sometimes referred to as an automatic rifle. It fires intermediate bullets – more powerful than a sub-machine gun, but less powerful than a standard semi-automatic/manually loaded rifle or a machine gun – out to an effective range of about 600 metres. It's a compromise weapon, designed to give infantrymen reasonably accurate sustained fire (or automatic) fire capability but also light enough to be easily portable.

Automatic carbine

Carbines are shorter, less powerful rifles. They are semi-automatic/self-loading rifles capable of firing one shot with each trigger pull. They were originally designed in the nineteenth century as manually operated weapons for cavalry/mounted infantry and artillerymen who found it impracticable to carry the standard rifle. The British short magazine Lee-Enfield (SMLE) rifle, introduced before the First World War, fused the carbine/rifle design into one weapon powerful enough for the infantryman and light enough for support troops. The carbine carried on in use into the twentieth century – famously the US M-1 carbine – but the advent of lighter rifles and then the assault rifle has overshadowed the carbine. There are smaller automatic carbine versions of the Kalashnikov used by Russian police force units and special protection teams.

Automatic pistol

No pistol is truly automatic. If it were, it would be regraded and called a sub-machine gun or a machine pistol. An 'automatic' pistol is a small hand-held firearm that is self-loading (or semi-automatic) in that each time a round is fired the weapon automatically ejects the spent cartridge shell, reloads another round into the chamber and re-cocks the weapon. Thus, it is ready to fire again. The system for doing this relies on the gas from the explosion of the cartridge to work back the moving parts. An automatic pistol is not the same as a revolver. The latter has a rotating barrel from which the rounds are taken and then fired. This is done manually by pressing the trigger and does not require the use of gas from the exploding bullet.

Automatic rifle

A standard rifle is not automatic. It is manual or semi-automatic/self-loading (semi-automatic and self-loading meaning the same thing). It fires one shot per trigger pull. Traditionally, rifle ammunition is large and powerful, designed to be effective at great range. With such powerful ammunition, it is very difficult to make an effective automatic rifle. You had either to use a heavier weapon – the machine gun – or use less powerful ammunition – the assault rifle. Semi-automatic rifles started to come into service in the 1930s.

Light machine gun
The light machine gun is capable of being fired by one man, usually from a bipod or from the hip in an emergency.

Locking apparatus
Apart from sub-machine guns and some pistols, all weapons – manual or automatic – need to have a device to lock the bullet into the breech (or chamber). Without such a mechanism the bullet will not be accurately propelled down the barrel and gas from the exploding bullet will burst out of the rear of the weapon. More then this, semi-automatic and automatic firing requires the gas from the explosion of the bullet to be channelled into a gas chamber. Without a proper locking mechanism that opens and closes the breech, efficiently ejecting the spent cartridge and loading a new round (or bullet), automatic/semi-automatic weapons will not work properly.

Muzzle break
A muzzle break is a mechanism at the tip of the barrel that controls and directs the gas escaping down the barrel after a bullet has been fired. Even with a gas chamber to collect the gas to be used in a rearward motion to reload the weapon, some gas will always escape out the barrel. This can cause difficulties as the force of the gas following each bullet out of the barrel can make the weapon hard to control. Indeed, in

the worst case the weapon will rise as it is being fired, making it inaccurate. The AK-47 does not have a muzzle break (it does have a nut); the AKM and AK-74 do have muzzle breaks.

Ordnance
Originally, a term used for guns/artillery, it is now also used as a general term for explosives and artillery shells, or munitions in whatever form.

Sub-machine gun
First used in 1915, the sub-machine gun is a light, short, portable automatic weapon designed to fire pistol ammunition. The calibre of such a weapon (i.e. the bullet used) is often larger than that of rifles or machine guns but the bullet fired is shorter and less propellant is used in the cartridge to fire the bullet. This allows for rapid fire with, usually, a simple breechblock mechanism that does not lock fully before each round is fired (often called a 'blowback' design). Often a big spring in the receiver directs the breechblock backwards and forwards. If a more powerful bullet were used with such a firing system, the result would be intolerable, as the extra power would make the weapon impossible to handle. Effective up to around 200 metres, the rounds fired from a sub-machine gun lose power rapidly and are not very accurate. Thus, such a weapon is only of much use for personal protection or close-quarter battle

Swivel lock
Swivel lock is another term used for the locking apparatus.

Matthew Hughes

BIOGRAPHICAL DETAILS

Year	*Age*	*Event (in Kalashnikov's life)*
1919		(10 November 1919) Birth of Mikhail Timoveyevich Kalashnikov, in Kurya (Altai region).
1930	11	Kalashnikov family deported to Siberia.
1934	15	First escape.
1936	17	Second escape.
1937	18	(1937–8) Technical secretary in the political sector of the 3rd section of the Turkestan-Siberia railway ('Turksib'), at Matai station.
1938	19	(September 1938 to June 1941) Military service in the Red Army at Stryi, Kiev military district, as tank driver and mechanic.
1939	20	(1939–40) Builds a metre to keep count of the number of times a tank is fired.
1940	21	Meeting with Zhukov, who gives him a watch.
1940	21	(1940–1) His 'tank-shot metre' goes into production in Leningrad; later, he builds a 'mass declutching' device.

1941	22	(July–October) Involved in combat; is wounded.
1941	22	(October 1941 to January 1942) Hospital.
1942	23	(January–July 1942) On convalescence leave after his wound; works alone on the design of a sub-machine gun at the Matai station (Kazakhstan).
1942	23	(July) The academician Blagonravov signs an attestation supporting the sub-machine gun designed by Kalashnikov (in Tashkent).
1942	23	(August 1942 to October 1944) Designer in the department of innovations of the military district of Central Asia.
1943	24	(March) Begins working on his light machine gun in Tashkent.
1943	24	(December) His light machine gun does not win the competition.
1944	25	(June–November) Building a rifle in Shurovo. Fails to win the competition.
1944	25	(October 1944 to September 1949) Designer in the department of innovations of the USSR Armed Forces at Kolomna.
1944	25	Invents a device adapted for use on the SG-43 machine gun which makes it possible to fire one shot at a time (still employed today).
1945	26	His assault rifle wins the competition of the Main Artillery Directorate.
1946	27	Starts working on the assault rifle the AK-46, at Kovrov.
1947	28	(July–August) Trials at the Shurovo Polygon.
1948	29	(January) The USSR Defence Ministry decides to launch production of the assault rifle at Izhevsk.

1949	30	(September 1949 until today) Designer at Izhevsk.
1949	30	Order of the Red Star.
1949	30	Stalin Prize, First Grade.
1949	30	The AK-47 assault rifle is officially approved.
1950	30	(March 1950 to June 1954) Deputy at the Supreme Soviet, 3rd legislature.
1957	38	Order of the Red Flag of Labour.
1958	39	Order of Lenin and Hammer and Sickle medal (Hero of Socialist Labour).
1959	40	His AKM and AKMS assault rifles are officially approved.
1959	40	His RPK light machine gun is officially approved.
1961	42	His PK and PKS machine guns are officially approved.
1962	43	His PKT and PKM machine guns are officially approved.
1964	45	Lenin Prize.
1966	47	(June 1966 to June 1970) Deputy at the Supreme Soviet, 7th legislature.
1969	50	Order of Lenin.
1970	51	(June 1970 to June 1974) Deputy at the Supreme Soviet, 8th legislature.
1971	52	Doctorate in technical sciences.
1974	55	(June 1974 to March 1979) Deputy at the Supreme Soviet, 9th legislature.
1974	55	Order of the October Revolution.
1974	55	The AK-74 and AKS-74 assault rifles are officially approved.
1974	55	The RPK-74 and RPKS-74 light machine guns are officially approved.
1976	57	(February) Delegate at the 25th Congress of the Soviet Union Communist Party.

1976	57	Order of Lenin and second Hammer and Sickle medal (Hero of Socialist Labour with two stars).
1979	60	(March 1979 to March 1984) Deputy at the Supreme Soviet, 10th legislature.
1979	60	(March 1979 to March 1984) Deputy at the Supreme Soviet, 10th legislature.
1979	60	His AKS-74U assault rifle is officially approved.
1982	63	Order of Friendship of Peoples.
1984	65	(March 1984 to April 1988) Deputy at the Supreme Soviet, 11th legislature.
1985	66	Order of the Patriotic War, First Grade.
1990	71	(May) Visit to the Smithsonian Institution (Edward Ezell), United States.
1991	72	(August) Visit to China. An accident leaves him half deaf.
1991	72	(October) Visit to Argentina.
1992	73	(April) Visits the Sturm, Roger & Co. firm (William B. Ruger), United States.
1992	73	(November) Visit to Finland.
1993	74	(January) The SHOT hunting salon (United States).
1993	74	(February) Weapons exhibition (United Arab Emirates).
1993	74	(March) Visit to Bulgaria.
1993	74	(March) Visit to the United Kingdom.
1994	75	(January) The SHOT hunting salon (United States).
1994	75	Order of Merit for the Motherland, Second Grade.
1994	75	Honorary member of the Russian Academy of Engineering Sciences.
1994	75	Appointed brigadier general.

1995	76	(February) Weapons exhibition (United Arab Emirates).
1995	76	(February) Weapons exhibition (Columbia).
1995	76	(March) Visit to Bulgaria.
1995	76	(September) Visit to Saudi Arabia.
1995	76	(December) Visit to France.
1996	77	(February) Visit to Iran.
1996	77	(May) Visit to Switzerland.
1996	77	(June) Weapons exhibition (France).
1996	77	Honorary member of the International Academy of Sciences, Industry, Education and Arts (United States).
1997	78	(April) Visit to India.
1997	78	Weapon of honour (pistol) presented by the President of the Russian Federation.
1998	79	Order of Saint Andrew.
1998	79	Prize of the Russian State.
1998	79	(October) Visit to the United States.
1999	80	Order of Honour (Byelorussia).
1999	80	Named divisional general.
2001	82	(June) Meets Qadhafi in Libya.
2001	82	Member of the Academy of Natural Sciences of Russia.
2002	83	(June) Weapons exhibition (France).
2002	83	(July) Visit to Germany, at the invitation of the *Land* of Thuringia.
2002	83	(October) Visit to Jordan.

SELECT BIBLIOGRAPHY AND FILMOGRAPHY

Books

Édouard Ducoureau, *Le Kalachnikov* (Paris: Éditions du Guépard, 1982) (in French).

Edward C. Ezell, *Kalashnikov, The Arms and the Man (The AK-47 Story)* (Cobourg, Ontario: Collector Grade Publications, 2001).

——— *The AK-47 Story. Evolution of the Kalashnikov Weapons* (Harrisburg, PA: Stackpole Books, 1988).

Mikhail T. Kalashnikov, *Zapiski konstruktora-oruzheinika* ('Notes of a Weapons Designer') (Moscow: Voyennoe Izdatelstvo, 1992) (in Russian).

——— *Ot chuzhogo poroga do Spasskykh vorot* ('From the threshold of a foreign house to the Spassky Gate') (Moscow: Voyennyi Parad, 1997) (in Russian),

——— *Ya s vami shel odnoi dorogoi* ('I have followed the same path as you') (Moscow: Vsia Rossia, 1999) (in Russian).

Aleksandr A. Malimon, *Otechestvennie avtomaty (Zapiski*

ispitatelia-oruzheinika) (Moscow: Ministerstvo Oborony Rossiiskoi Federatsii, 1999) (in Russian).

Aleksei Nedelin, *Kalashnikov Arms* (Moscow: Voyennyi Parad, 1999) (bilingual edition, Russian-English).

Documentary films

Gilles du Jonchay, *Les Années Kalachnikov*, France 3/IMA Productions, 1993.

Axel Engstfeld and Herbert Itabersack, *Le Kalachnikov*, WDR/ORF/Arte, 2000.

INDEX

Made in the USA
Monee, IL
05 February 2023

27142499R10115